The
SECRET
GARDENS
of
FRANCE

The SECRET GARDENS *of* FRANCE

MIRABEL OSLER

PAVILION

First published in Great Britain in 1992 by
PAVILION BOOKS LIMITED
26 Upper Ground, London SE1 9PD

Text copyright © Mirabel Osler 1992
Photographs copyright © Georges Lévêque 1992

The moral right of the author has been asserted

Designed by Janet James

A CIP catalogue record for this book
is available from The British Library

ISBN 1 85793 311 7
Printed and bound in Hong Kong

2 4 6 8 10 9 7 5 3 1

This book may be ordered by post
direct from the publisher. Please
contact the Marketing Department.
But try your bookshop first.

Frontispiece: Catherine Vercken's garden in Burgundy.

CONTENTS

An Impossible Quest 7

*S*ENSITIVE *L*ADIES

*S*OME *I*RREPRESSIBLE *G*ARDENERS

*J*ARDINS *R*AFFINÉS

*L*ES *J*ARDINS DU *T*EMPS *P*ASSÉ

*C*EREBAL *G*ARDENERS

An Impossible Quest

If gardens are the one area available to each of us in which to create our own personal visions of paradise – why should the French be excluded? We know about England. We are annually bombarded by such a plethora of garden books inciting us to consider Form, Design, Patterns and Scent – the Classic, the Country and the English garden – that we browse through pages of photographs, become engrossed by captions, but in the end fail to distinguish one book from another. I know the British are said to be the only ones, that our garden style infiltrates to all five continents, but what happens just across the water? I wanted to find out.

About sixty million years ago a vast upheaval took place in France, which threw up the Alps to the south-east and the Pyrenees to the south-west, leaving the immense limestone tableland of the Massif Central where deep fissures fractured the rock to form valleys and turbulent water courses. Rivers flowed like life-giving arteries through the land mass of France; they passed from eroded uplands to pastoral sweetness, from forested desolation to marshy wilderness. And in between? In between, I felt sure, the French with all those centuries of creativity behind them must surely have made gardens sequestered and unfamiliar. The provocation was irresistible.

I was after French gardeners – not British ones – who were making gardens with their own imprint, where attitudes and ambitions would have a distinct Gallic urbanity. The French passion for amputating trees, which makes the Romantic gardener wince, has passed down the centuries to the present day, when orderly plantings line the roads and decapitated trees form mutilated verticals in public gardens. My empathy had been aroused from the start when I discovered that what we call a 'Ha-ha', the French call an 'Ah-ah'. Somehow there was a whimsical knowingness about the French way of pronouncing the word.

The discouragement I received was universal. Wet blankets were dumped on me from every expert francophile, every travelled gardener, every enlightened friend. 'France – and gardens? Forget it!' Or else the cynical snort: 'You're mad. The French and gardens? God, if they can't eat

Part of the young garden on the Lake of Geneva belonging to
Yves and Anne-Monique d'Yvoire.

it, they won't grow it!' Only doctors, dentists and *notaires*, I was told, made gardens. Thank you, thank you. Unadulterated negativity is a potent incentive. Your advice was invaluable.

And in a superficial way they were right; for the traveller passing through, French gardens do not exist, except for those mounds with a house on top, and drooping conifers and shrubs dotting the slopes. But only up to a point. When you read of the gardens contained in this book, you will have to reconsider that sweeping condemnation which was continually thrown at me: '*What* French gardens?'

There was another incentive for the book. I longed to let the voice of each gardener have as much definition as the flowers they planted. How can a garden and its gardener be separated – the one area highlighted, the other left shadowy? And yet book after book takes you through the layout, the design, the pH content of the soil; every plant is hammered home, every colour and height scrupulously recorded; but where, in these gardens, are the gardeners? Hidden behind their flowers, unfortunately. Yet they are the creators; their sensitivity, adroitness, philosophy, moods or dedication are as indispensable and deeply rooted in their gardens as a tap-root is to the crown of a tree. But why do we not hear from them? So although I do go on rather, in certain of my French gardens, with the naming of plants, I still hope that the gardeners themselves shine through with their inimitable egos. For one thing became clear, as I researched this book: French gardeners were far more generous and responsive in giving me their help and time than I had been led to expect by all the knowing cynicism I was offered before I set out.

As I was not looking for the renowned gardens of other centuries, or for the fine gardens already well known from *Private Gardens of France* and *French Garden Style*, and did not want to rely on Michel Racine's *Le Guide des Jardins de France*, my search for French gardens depended on instinct, not logic; so, to begin with, my suppositions were generated in the very nebulous region of my imagination.

Knowing that the climate of France possesses a diversity of extremes way beyond anything we have in England, my idea of what I might find there was limitless. I imagined finding coastal gardens contorted by prevailing winds, and bizarre exotics thriving in balmy humidity. On lake sides and river banks I hoped to discover boggy havens, and behind town walls there would be retreats of austere tranquility. Would I find gardens above the snow-line in the Savoie and Dauphiné – a region described so evocatively in a Michelin guide as having *un caractère farouche*? In the

Auvergne, where one or two million years ago now-dormant volcanoes spewed molten lava, incinerating the forest to wood-coal, would there be gardens growing among the skeletons of mastodons and sabre-toothed tigers, with flowers nourished on volcanic detritus?

I had no defined frontiers to the sort of garden I was looking for, but I hoped to unearth not only flower gardens, but parterres on a domestic scale (rather than those seen at Courances or Vaux-le-Vicomte). I know such places can be found in municipal parks. In Bourganeuf in the Creuse, for instance, there is a tiny enclosure beside the Tour de Zizim where an exemplary parterre is touchingly maintained, but for whom? The garden is too diminutive to walk in, yet it remains there year after year as a small French statement.

Gardens without flowers, which the French achieve with such masterly ease, where their skill with the shears creates pared and pure places in contrast to our romantic prodigality, were what I anticipated. I was not disappointed. In the Dordogne there is a green garden of such rigorous delicacy and distinguished architectural perfection it takes your breath away. And it is open to the public. The Manoir d'Eyrignac belongs to Monsieur Sermadiras de Pouzols de Lile. Its diminishing alley of hornbeam buttresses and black-green cylinders of yew is of such precision it is hard to believe that the plants are all hand clipped, and the accuracy ensured by use of that simple device, a plumb line. I mention it here because it is a brilliant example of fastidious gardening most eloquently expressed.

And nurseries? Once French nurseries were abysmal places selling only bedding plants and conifers in a fairly peaky state of health. Would I find, these days, a widening of horizons? One gardener said to me, 'Nursery-men? They are not true gardeners! Most nurserymen have very ordinary things – they never search!' But a contrary opinion was given by another distinguished gardener: 'Now that people are wanting to create gardens, although they don't have ideas and they don't know about gardens, nurseries are beginning to flourish.'

This is true. For example, between Cahors and Puy-l'Evêque is a notable nursery: Pépinières Prayssacoises, belonging to Pierre Coffre, who spent a year at Hillier's. He showed us round a large collection of trees and open-ended tunnels of black netting which allow plenty of air to circulate and make a cool, shadowless refuge for seedlings. Other tunnels, made from plastic, are hot and humid to nurture fig, olive, lemon and banana trees. He grows bougainvilleas, a mass of hortensias and a beautiful rose I have never seen before: 'Ghislaine de Féligonde', draped over a fence, is covered with buds the warm colour of cornelians and has tousled flowers fading to the delicacy of an apricot milkshake. The collection of shrubs and flowers radiates good health. Anyone living in the Lot who wants to make a garden has a head-start with Pépinières Prayssacoises on their doorstep.

Then there are kitchen gardens. *Potagers* are intrinsic to France. Drive anywhere in the country, and in no time you will see examples of the French talent for prim uniformity from purple-leafed cabbages veined with crimson, lettuces the size of caliphs' turbans and blue leeks set out in rows of meticulous precision. At their most fastidious they are not only practical, but a scrupulous art form as well. France excels in this, as she does in municipal gardens full of garish embroidery. Both benefit from the French mania for control; for their geometric eye and native lust for docking every sprig of wayward greenery. In spite of Madame Vercken's cry, from her garden in Burgundy '. . . I love organizing plants, the roses, but – how I should like to disorganize', long may this instinctive Gallic deftness last. The results are fabulous. Who wants us all to sing in the same key? Our romantic turmoil, seen in summer borders heaving with luxuriance, is perfection, but when I come to France I am dead set on discipline.

Kitchen gardens are as old as the fourth millenium BC. In France the most illustrious must be that of Villandry, with its reconstructed ornamental layout based on sixteenth-century engravings, where graphic patterns are embellished with bright explosions from standard roses. But on this journey it was not the splendour of these great *potagers* which was compelling. I wanted to find the same conformity in more humble surroundings.

The possibilities seemed limitless; all I needed to do was start.

One of my first sources of information was David Wheeler, editor and publisher of the gardening journal *Hortus*. His introductions to French experts in various fields opened innumerable doors. Then the garden photographer Jerry Harpur gave me invaluable addresses of French garden designers and landscape architects, to whom I wrote. Another early directive came by way of Richard Binns, that highly informative and prolific author of guide books to eating and staying in France. Although gardens are not his thing, he was most generous in giving me the names of particular cronies in the world of restaurateurs, who might know of gardens in their locality. Each introduction I was given was worth pursuing. Some led nowhere, others were unexpectedly productive. Letter followed letter to France, in an effort to find the kind of gardens I was looking for.

Two of the seventeenth-century gates at the sad garden of Moutier Saint-Jean belonging to Col Challan Belval.

Throughout my search two names came up over and over again: la Baronne de Waldner and the late Vicomte de Noailles; but their magnificent gardens are hardly 'unknown', nor are some others which were also recommended. Equally, two or three of those I have included only just come into the category of 'hidden' gardens. Some can be visited by the public, one or two can be seen by appointment. And several of the gardens I found without prior introductions – the courtyard at St Vrain, the *potager* at Berzé-le-Chatel, the kitsch garden in the Lot – and so on.

One immovable date, around which everything else pivoted, was Courson. The advice I was given to visit the biannual Flower Show, held in May and October, proved indispensable. Here, I was told, I would find garden designers, landscape architects, botanists, writers, photographers, amateur gardeners and nursery owners from every province of France.

The seventeenth-century château at Courson-Monteloup, thirty-five kilometres from Paris, is approached by an imposing *allée*. Approximately forty hectares of parkland, where more than a thousand trees and flowering shrubs have been planted, and with a lake surrounded by azaleas and rhododendrons, is the setting for the three days of the show, *les journées des plantes*.

The Flower Show, first started in 1980, is held at the back of what once were the stables – a long and imposing building with a beautiful tiled floor, at one side of the château courtyard. Walk through the stables, past an enormous display of gardening books from *La Maison Rustique*, and you find yourself in a gardener's dream of paradise – a kind of floral disorder under stately chestnut and maple trees, where flowers are dumped on the grass in great generous and uncontrived armfuls. Flowers are stuffed into packing cases, restrained by baulks of timber, generally shown off with the casual nonchalance of people dedicated to displaying their plants, not their sophisticated or cunning flair for dramatization.

I saw droves of pelargoniums gathered in a mass of fluttering petals; sumptuous fuchsias grouped like crimson and purple bolts of rich cloth; hydrangeas lying like a pool of undulating mauve and blue waves. Nothing was elaborately composed or theatrically presented, nor need you have your wits about you in case Cilla Black turned out to be, not a delightful little bulb, but a TV 'star' with particularly long legs, come to be photographed against a prize tiger-lily.

I was enchanted by Courson. I could not believe such ingenuousness existed in the jostling, cut-throat world of plant salesmen. Even so, some gardeners I spoke to were already lamenting the loss of the early years of innocence. 'It used to be a lot more intimate. Now it's getting commercial.

But then, I was very disappointed last time I went to the Chelsea Flower Show in London. I don't want to go again. I don't understand why so many people go – Chelsea is so artificial.' To me, coming to it for the first time, Courson appeared fresh and spontaneous. To walk in sunlight among displays of orchids, alpines, ferns, ornamental vegetables and medicinal plants, all standing hugger-mugger on the ground backed by the distant grandeur of parkland, seemed to me to be the fulfilment of an ideal flower show. And as far as I was concerned, it also provided a unique genus of garden experts.

Some of the most helpful people I met were members of the *Association des Parcs Botaniques de France*. The APBF was first started by a small group of owners of botanical gardens and arboreta with the aim of safeguarding what was already in existence, and also of rousing others to make their own collections. They wanted to highlight France's horticultural heritage: that classic seventeenth-century heritage described by Marina Schinz in *Visions of Paradise* as having been built 'with arrogance and armies', when whole villages were demolished, swamps were drained and hills reshaped to make way for gardens on such a gargantuan scale that the human form was reduced to a mote. The Association also initiated an inventory of the numerous species introduced into France; they promoted discussions on conservation; they arranged visits to each other's gardens, and sought out new ones. As well, they produced their own newsletter. Some members were scientific while others were amateur enthusiasts, and those I met at Courson were wonderful. Their invaluable advice pointed me towards some of the most superb gardens I visited.

The atmosphere at Courson was of such informal friendliness that people came carrying plastic bags with ailing roses as they anxiously sought advice on a bad bout of blackspot, twigs with cankerous nodules, or recalcitrant buds refusing to blossom. Benevolence reigned. Other visitors came from as far away as Holland, Germany or Belgium. With them they brought plants from their own gardens and held impromptu car-boot sales before loading up with new plants from Courson. Unlike other flower shows, throughout the three-day event everything was for sale. In the shade, hidden among the trees, were trucks loaded with replacements, and I was told that each evening a floral romp took place among the visitors staying in the surrounding hotels, where they exchanged or bartered for plants in a frenzy of volatile trading.

I cannot leave the subject of Courson without mentioning one most crucial encounter. This was with Louis Benech, a young and distinguished garden designer who is involved in the prestigious job of replanting the

Tuileries – those gardens in Paris first created by Catherine de Medici in the sixteenth century. He sat down with us on a bench amid the teeming throng of nursery gardeners setting up their displays on the day before the show opened, and steadily went through his address book giving us names of gardeners, in spite of numerous interruptions and demands for his attention. And it was he who tentatively, almost as an afterthought, and after sizing us up, gave us the name of an island where the two reclusive brothers Paul and Jean live. When you have read the chapter in which they appear, you will understand why I am so deeply indebted to Louis Benech.

My companions on the journey were my daughter Tamsin, who is an excellent French speaker, and her seven-month-old daughter, Cassandra. It sounds insane, I know, to make a journey criss-crossing France for five thousand miles with a baby. But although having a creature with strong demands of her own slowed us up a good deal, the responsive welcomes and the loosening of formalities as she caused mild turmoil along the way did add another dimension to our travelling. Gallic proprieties, which might otherwise have taken weeks to thaw, dissolved instantly.

The book is not chronologically laid out to follow the route we took during six weeks' travelling in May and June; instead, the chapters are loosely grouped according to the personalities of the gardeners and their gardens. This means there is no logical progression as you read from chapter to chapter. The method may madden those with an instinctive sense of direction as we seem to flit insanely about the map of France.

May in France is a lyrical month; it begins with the custom of giving bunches of *muguet* – the lily of the valley – followed not many days later by the song of nightingales. Larks and nightingales pursued us throughout the countryside. And once, unexpectedly in Burgundy, we heard the reedy voice of cicadas. We were told they had only appeared in this part of France in the last three years, having been brought in cars by hunters from the south when they came to shoot in winter. May is also the month when village houses are underlined by a stroke of irises the filmy blue of sky after rain; it is the month of Madonna lilies and of weed-killer – that brutal pogrom carried on against anything living such as charlock, wild lupins and of course small poppies. The *coquelicot* – which is said to open when the cock crows – is almost the definitive flower of France. In one narrow valley flowers flowed like a tide of scarlet, tapering away into the distance so that I would not have been surprised to see a swimmer doing breast-stroke through them. Guelder roses crowded the hedgerows; orchids, pink bush vetch and shepherd's purse grew along the verges of fields whose crops

One of the pools at the nursery garden, Planbessin in Normandy.

were undiscernible as they drowned in yellow buttercups sprinkled with ox-eye daisies. Stonecrop, house-leeks, rusty-backed and hart's tongue ferns trickled over roofs and in the cracks of walls, together with loosely meandering threads of ivy-leaved toadflax, that commonplace vagrant which strays so prettily. When you are in France in May you have no doubt that you have come at the right time of year: when you are there in October the same thoughts occur with the same conviction.

As we travelled, certain observations had a forceful, if sometimes transitory, impact; yet I should like to record them merely because they did seem noteworthy at the time. For instance, somewhere around mid-May all the ladies in the villages or countryside we passed through started wearing straw hats. Their appearance was an immediate signal that, whatever the weather, we must be on the brink of summer. Less alluring was the fashion for padded shoulders. Stylish ladies bending forward to point out a plant in their gardens needed to quickly hoick back their shoulder pads as they stood up, or be left standing with curious deformities.

Another trivial observation was how French gardeners seem to use gravel as we in England use pre-cast concrete paving. Gravel was everywhere. It was the universal choice whether the gardens were in Picardy or Roussillon, in the Vendée or on the shores of Lac Léman. This seemed curious, considering the many sources of varied and different-coloured stone in France. But how refreshing it was occasionally to find, in the arid parts of southern France where rain may not fall for months, the restful use of paving replacing grass. The world-wide addiction to lawns can sometimes be carried to extremes. In Greece the snobbish owner of a villa will go to any lengths to bring in tankers of water to maintain a vivid patch of Irish green, ignoring the possibilities for making an indigenous Mediterranean garden. In the Far East, British consuls in unlikely places will cravenly copy their Embassies in an effort to keep up the verdurous tradition surrounding a statue of Queen Victoria, in spite of water shortages during the hot season. So when in France we discovered gardeners who had abandoned any ambition to sustain a *pelouse*, we found often that they had created such shady havens of repose, from stone and shadows, that the word 'garden' took on another dimension.

Among the great gardening disasters of France, far from trivial, are swimming pools. In a commercial brochure on *piscines*, not one of the eight pages of photographs offers anything but turquoise. There is no suggestion that alternatives exist. These swimming pools – and they abound in French gardens – annihilate the most beautiful places in one fell, lethal swoop – in fact, the more beautiful the garden, the more outrageous these *piscines* appear. How can gardeners allow it? It hardly seems possible. Where are their eyes and their sense of harmony? With all their feeling for flowers, colours and design, are gardeners imperceptive to what they have done in using a colour that does not even exist in nature? Instead, the vicious lustre is allowed to take centre-stage while all the other colours just vanish off the set. In all the gardens we saw, we found only one owner with a sufficiently discerning eye to have solved the problem of this universal disfigurement. As water in a pool is naturally blue, by painting the sides yellow he had turned his pool into a harmonious green. It was a simple solution to an unforgivable form of garden abuse.

One very eminent gardener who spoke English fluently remarked that 'The French language is not good for describing flowers. You have simple words in English. French is a rich language, but it is too deliberate for the garden, for the flowers, for nature.' Not being bilingual as she was, I could not comment, but in gardens, too, such deliberation is certainly inherent. Letting go in a garden, in the right places, seems almost a physical impossibility with French gardeners. Where, in several flawless gardens, there was a wilder, more spirited or uncontrived area, still the grass was evenly shorn. In England the gardener would perhaps have allowed wild flowers to seed, or have cut the grass varying lengths to add a green design under trees. When I commented on this the French gardener would invariably explain that it would be such a lot of work. Yes, yes – of course it would. And yet in the rest of the garden they worked tirelessly, expending hours of trouble to achieve the faultless effect; the subtleties and artistry were refined to perfection. It was as though the parts of the garden which were not formal or laid out with flowers did not belong to serious gardening; as if time spent on informality was time squandered.

Russell Page wrote in *The Education of a Gardener*, when talking about the many grand commissions he undertook: 'Each year I spent periods of weeks and sometimes months in France. I was fascinated by this contact with a definite and stylized culture new to me and clearer and sharper than the English tradition which has absorbed and modified and welded together influences from so many different countries . . .' Most pertinently he went on to say: 'In France foreign importations, whether of style or material, had only (it seemed to me) been absorbed if and when they could conform to French style.' *When they could conform to French style*! Oh, but of course – long may it last.

Later he wrote: 'Gardening in England seems like a slow process of wooing growing things into giving their best. There is no finality and there would be no satisfaction if there were. In France, the contrary would seem to be true. A pleasure garden since the time of du Cerceau [architect and engraver, whose engravings were a source of sixteenth-century French garden design] or earlier has been a formal pattern laid out like a carpet; it extends the formalities of the salon into the open air. A "green drawing-room" or the "shade-room", a "theatre of greenery", inevitable parts of a classical garden composition, express the nature of a French garden quite precisely. That great designer Le Nôtre, however vast and ingenious his schemes, seldom departed from this rigid concept. Measure and clarity are essential to the French garden scene.'

Though they may be modest compared with some of those he designed and planted, I feel that if Russell Page were to visit today some of the gardens contained in this book he would perhaps be astonished and pleased to discover just how deviant, innovative and personally idiosyncratic some French gardeners have become. Yet examples of the style he wrote about in his book can still be found in many contemporary gardens, whether they are on a grand scale or not. Looking at French gardens, I feel more than ever that they prove there are no 'right' ways of gardening – only alternatives.

SENSITIVE
LADIES

'MAIS, MAMAN – AH, CE JARDIN!

In the heart of Burgundy, in rolling countryside where poppies and charlock flank the roads and the land has been farmed for centuries, is a serene garden. It lies on the outskirts of a village taken over by peonies, tamarisks and honeysuckle, with swallows skimming low among the houses. Here Catherine Vercken spends eight months of each year, tending and cherishing her shrubs and flowers, filling her days with floral endeavour.

In her reply to my request to visit her Madame Vercken had written, '*Mon jardin est assez simple mais j'espère qu'au moment de votre passage il sera en bonne forme.*' Such a gentle statement turned out to be indicative of the very voice of both the garden and the gardener. On our way there I had tried to eradicate any template from my mind of how most French gardens appear so that I could free-fall into her garden with a mind vacant of preconceptions.

It was early May; wisteria and roses festooned doorways, logs were still piled up under the eaves of houses as evidence that the past winter had been a mild one, and in the valley of the Armançon a woman wearing a sea-green straw hat stood fishing in the river, a sign surely that summer had now arrived?

Burgundy is a large and seemingly ill-defined region; it conjures up Romanesque and Gothic architecture, grand dukes and abbeys, Charollais cows and wine. But for Catherine Vercken and her garden, what counts is the gigantic puckering of the earth which took place about fifty million years ago and left her with barely enough topsoil to grow a rose. Overwhelming heat in summer, when the shallow soil makes watering a constant chore, and winters when the cold falls like a dead weight across the region mean that growing things from seed is barely possible. She laments the lack of snow for its protection; instead, when the dry, freezing cold lasts for weeks she admits that every year, when she returns from spending the winter in Paris, 'I have plants that disappear, that die.'

Madame Vercken spent her childhood in the village; her parents had a house lower down beside the church. 'The most beautiful gardens are old –

PREVIOUS PAGE
Catherine Vercken's garden flows into the countryside.

in them the trees and shrubs are magnificent. My parents' garden was a true old garden – mine is still young.' (Twenty-five years old!) Three of her daughters were married from the house and when one of her sons, who had been born in the village, asked if he could live in the house below her garden, his mother agreed but only on condition that there should be no fence between them so that the children should be free to roam from one garden to another. This attitude towards her children and her seventeen grandchildren exemplifies how Catherine Vercken treats her garden: with loving tolerance and no boundaries.

The garden, made out of sloping land dropping down towards the valley, flows with instinctive movement. 'I followed the contours – you know – the same paths the game birds took.' To begin with, nothing is visible from the threshold of the house except the gravel terrace with troughs and plants around the door. Walking to the low stone parapet you are quite unprepared for what confronts you – a view of unbelievable tranquillity, where smudgy-coloured tones of distant hills, meadows washed with poppies, and lines of poplars making vertical emphasis blend harmoniously from the garden to the horizon. The sheer sensual pleasure of a garden and landscape that run seamless to the sky make you realize you are in a garden of fine-grained sensitivity.

Dark purple roses, white wisteria, clematis and lady's mantle, senecios, pinky tulips and delphiniums stray in seemingly artless abandon. '*Mon mélange n'est absolument pas intellectuel*, but where there's space, in it goes and it more or less works,' is how Catherine Vercken describes her philosophy of gardening. 'The children pull up something – it happens – maybe an iris, I replant it quickly without knowing its colour or where it came from. And that's how I am always finding surprises in my flower-beds.' Or, having lifted the irises, she panics and hurriedly plants them wherever she can find space, 'So that they don't die on me. In the end they take, and then I no longer dare lift them again – nor do I know their colour – I have forgotten.' She explains with good humour, 'Sometimes I see something in flower and think, "but that's horrible. What on earth is that thing doing there? How is it that I put it in such a place?" But I didn't – well I put it there to prevent it from dying!' When she comes across tulips as she is digging she puts them in her pocket, 'but I can't leave them there so one day I plant them and that way I see things that I haven't planned. Sometimes it's a success, other times not. There are always surprises!'

Catherine Vercken's garden, its very fabric reflecting the person, has all been grown from cuttings or seeds. Nothing was transplanted from a container, nothing was uprooted from a nursery or bought in the market. As she says herself: '*Mon jardin n'est fait que de boutures ou de semis, ce qui ne le fait pas encore glorieux!*' (Made only from cuttings or seeds, it's still got a long way to go!). She gathers cuttings from whatever source pleases her and has the patience and dexterity to make them thrive. From her own roses she plans to take more cuttings so as to extend their density; in England, where she often goes to visit one of her daughters who lives there, 'I am always tempted. I can't help myself! Look, that little cutting came from Wales, and that rose, 'Iceberg', from Gloucestershire.' From London she also brought back seeds, and others have been sent to her from America, but more often than not they are a failure. 'I am always on the lookout for unusual seeds which aren't too banal. I don't have many because it is so difficult – I sow in a cold frame and hope they will be tough; resist the cold, heat, the drought and even the rain because sometimes it rains and when it starts it rains enormously.' But after two or three attempts at growing something, without rancour she accepts defeat.

When she started there was no garden and the house was a hovel. All the coarse undergrowth had to be pulled up bit by bit while year by year she planted more things. She spends about two thousand francs a year on the garden, and as she does the garden entirely herself she can, sadly, no longer keep up her *potager* – 'I loved it very much.' She had intended to replace the vegetable garden with grass. 'But well, it is not at all the same – no, no, it becomes then something banal whereas my *potager* – oh, it was a corner that I adored!'

From the terrace flights of small steps lead down to more terraces. These are magical; there are minute mown lawns all shadowy from gnarled fruit trees where irises as pale as the 'whites' of babies' eyes flow like blue brush strokes along the mellowed stones holding up the banks. Yet Madame Vercken longs for more room. 'Of course one always dreams of all those big magnificent gardens. For a truly beautiful garden you need space.' I could not agree with her. Looking round, I saw her *Hydrangea paniculata*, which in late summer will have masses of pyramidal white flowers turning pinkish as they age, 'Albertine', that vigorous climbing rose covered with thorns and coppery flowers which defy description because in whatever part of the country you find this rose it always seems to have taken on a slightly different hue, the '*feuille de chêne*' hydrangea (*H. quercifolia*) whose leaves in autumn turn to burnished crimson; I saw her blue caryopteris and delphiniums, the white clematis 'Marie Boisselot' and all the sweet-smelling geraniums. It did not look to the outsider as though the garden was in any way frustrated. Only the gardener herself felt the restraint.

One of Mme Vercken's shadowy terraces built beneath the house.

'Seven or eight gardens is what I have but how can I separate one garden from the next? No garden should be seen at one glance.'

Yet through constant ingenuity this is just the effect she has achieved; each part, though on a diminutive scale, is indeed hidden from the next. 'You see I have a very pretty peony there – behind the pine tree? Good. It isn't visible. Only if you follow that path upwards, you aren't expecting it – then *voilà* – you discover such a pretty plant.' In another of her gardens, concealed in a corner, are poppies of such singular, smoky-mauve tones you might expect to find the colour in a piece of Fortuny silk rather than in a May-blooming *Papaver*.

Viburnum plicatum 'Mariesii' spreads its branches covered with tiny-petalled creamy flowers like layers of out-stretched fingers, and half hides wooden seats and a table. The colour of the furniture is like the shadowy bits of olive trees; no white, jarring and intrusive, wrecks this secluded corner. Here, on a still day when the heat of summer lies like a pall on the countryside, is a place to escape to, where Catherine Vercken can sit amid tactile and visual contentment. In another of the small gardens is a stone seat where two could carry on a *tête-à-tête*. The seat is made from some of the flat stone slabs which were once the roof of the house. Now they are used about the garden, as scraps of cotton are utilized in a patchwork quilt, to make terraces and paths which contrast so well with the mown grass.

At the back of the house Madame Vercken led us to her dahlia bed. In August it would be explosive. 'I had seen at Hampton Court – you know, as one leaves there's an enormous bed – the dahlias are all mixed up. I had such cheek. I said to myself, "I must have that!" Here, last year, it was fantastic – dahlias of all colours, some beautiful, some large – all mixed! It's more violent than choosing one colour.' But her unerring eye made her hide the dahlias away at the back of the house. As she explained: 'One has to come up here to see them. To have them all day long confronting you – oh no . . !'

Walking with her in late afternoon when the shadows were long, there was something wistful and rather plaintive about her garden. She loves every inch; she sees it as a young garden with everything still on the move, and yet I felt she had too few companions to share her quiet passion. 'All this I have created myself, nobody helps. I leave a little wildness at the same time as making something which is *soigné – j'arrive à laisser un peu de liberté tout en faisant quelques choses qui est soigné*. She pointed to a patch of grass she had roughly mown and then, almost as if she were speaking to herself, she said, 'It is very difficult with a wild garden – there is so much choice. Is that grass going to be good like that? And how far? Perhaps that little piece there would be better removed? And . . . well, moreover . . . well me, I'm French. I don't have that feeling naturally. My designs are always organized. Unfortunately I love organizing plants, the roses but – how I should like to disorganize!'

Looking at her Judas Tree, *Cercis siliquastrum*, grown from seed, whose bright rosy-lilac flowers bloom in clusters before the roundish leaves appear, she said, 'I make lists of things to be done each day so that my children tease me: "*Mais, Maman – ah ce jardin –* leave it!". But how can I? My family doesn't understand me except for my daughter in America, who has someone working for her. But that's absolutely not the same thing.'

Referring to English gardens and their influence on her, she admitted how she constantly read gardening books, acknowledging that England was the reference point, but that if she could go beyond, and create something which was not a copy of what is done there, she would find that infinitely preferable. Ten or so little cypress trees, which she had just sown in pots, would one day give strength to the distance. Then, tentatively, she went on to qualify her decision. 'One must be reasonable and encourage the things that really grow well in the region – if it is too eccentric, it's not good. One must limit one's ambitions.' Her comment was almost an understatement. No novelties, exotics or alien discord intruded anywhere. I was aware only of a garden, calm and unobtrusive, where the owner's hesitancy pervaded each one of her eight little gardens, where you felt every plant had been put there with a sensitive reticence.

'The garden is an art form; an expression of one's own desire in which I don't always believe,' Madame Vercken said as we sat having tea in a pretty cottagey room full of books. 'I ask myself, "Really, is it good? Isn't it completely mad – gardening serves no useful purpose?" And then I doubt. I doubt what I have created. I ask myself, "is it really worth casting a *coup d'oeil* at that? Or that . . . or that?" Yet to have someone encouraging you, who tells you, "It *is* good," or, "*Ce n'est pas mal*!" Well that indeed would do me good!'

Much later on our journey I came across again the same stoic philosophy towards gardening that Catherine Vercken has: 'I believe that everything one wishes to survive, even if it doesn't really belong to the region, has to be sown once. Either it'll work or not at all, in which case – *tant pis.*'

'LET YOURSELF BE LED
BY THE NOSE!'

'You'd better go soon – her baby is due any day.' This urgent advice to visit Madame Anne Simonet's garden was given to us by Louisa Dupont, who was an invaluable source of information on gardens in the Midi. 'Happy the Midi!' declared Colette, who wrote so passionately, and observed so lovingly every detail of flowers, herbs and trees. 'As early as January, it has the jonquil, the almond tree, the mimosa in great yellow clouds, the rustic carnation, and the anemone, while the rest of France is still stiff with cold.'

But it had not been quite like that for us. All the time, heading south, we had visions of fulgent abutilons, camellias and the grey-leafed cistus; of warmth, clear light and shallow-tiled roofs; olive, cypress, and lemon trees; bougainvillea and imposing umbrella pines. We expected to find market stalls sagging under the produce of fecund gardens. Shoals of small artichokes and young broad beans, willowy asparagus and carrots as slender as a finger would surround cherries piled in small crimson mountains, each one reflecting a paring of light; and thankfully cabbages would be an outrage of the past, belonging to Burgundy and the Savoie where the approach of early summer had still been retarded.

Instead we found hell. The Drôme, midway between Lyon and Marseilles, was a kind of man-made purgatory where chemical works, refineries and mineral beds, nuclear industry and hydro-electric power stations spewed their pollution into the upper atmosphere. Could we be near where Madame de Sévigné stayed with her daughter, relishing the figs and melons of Provence? Where Petrarch first saw Laura?

Our disillusionment was confirmed as we drove through torrential rain, at times so violent that motorists were forced to a standstill on the verges of the roads as hailstones clattered in a demonic frenzy against the cars, and the road afterwards was deep in white marbles that slid perilously under our tyres.

What a paradox, then, to be looking in the country of *usines atomiques* for a young woman who grew flowers in pots solely for the pleasure of their scents. What foresight, what perversity, and how intriguing. When absurd

The gateway leading from the village lane into
Anne Simonet's aromatic courtyard.

extremes present themselves like this, it does add a certain sparkle and zest to the occasion. Yet as we approached the hill village under a threatening sky my sense of the absurdity wavered and only Tamsin's determination kept us going. But of course I should not have been dispirited by a few nuclear power stations within smelling distance. Though Madame Simonet's garden was not much bigger than a couple of boardroom tables, what she grew there was a bees' paradise. We had discovered an exceptional gardener who distilled the fragrance from pots of flowers grown with an unfaltering commitment and a very green thumb.

The courtyard was private and quiet although we had just walked in from a narrow lane in the village; the massive wooden doors between high walls had been painted with *l'huile de lin* and turpentine mixed with blue powder and drawn along the grain of the wood which showed through, causing variations of blueness. The effect was of ancient weathering where the intensity of blue had lost its edge so that it harmonized with three lavender-blue chairs around a small table.

With her young son leaning against her, Madame Simonet spoke first of her lime tree: around the time of the summer solstice is when the leaves and flowers should be picked to make *tisane*. This aged tree, towering above the low roof of the house where the rare shaft of sunshine caused stippled shadows, was obviously of monumental importance to her and her husband. Other people might have banished the tree, needing the valuable space for flowers and shrubs, but in spite of its overwhelming presence, its shade and the fact that when they had arrived here three years previously the lime had been ailing, the first thing they undertook was to bring the tree back to health.

Pointing to the lime tree, Madame Simonet explained with pride how she and her husband had tackled the problem of their dying tree. 'It had been in such a sick state before and so brutally pruned, we decided to make a *couronne de fertilisation*, you understand? That's how we fed it.' First they had dug up the earth all around the tree, making a large circular channel in which they laid curved tiles, each one pierced in several places. After putting back the earth they kept an opening to each hole through which they could fertilize and water the roots. It was a patient and dedicated treatment. 'We have done the repruning,' Madame Simonet went on, pointing to the dense foliage still the transparent green of early summer, 'so now, you understand, it only needs *une petite toilette* now and then.'

We stood beside Anne Simonet as she pointed out her plants, pinching the leaves and smelling her fingers as she bent to touch each one with concentrated tenderness. (Some readers may want to skip this bit because ahead is a lot of Latin.) Of her twenty-five different scented geraniums she told us of her favourites: a velvety-leafed *Pelargonium tomentosum* for its penetrating minty smell; a small, white-flowered *P. odoratissimum* with silky, apple-scented leaves; a slender pink *P. crispum* from South Africa with a scent like lemon balm and a white *P.* x *fragrans* with red veins on the upper petals, and heart-shaped leaves redolent of nutmeg.

Crowded among groups of flowers where she intentionally keeps the colours to blue, violet, mauve, rose or white were other pelargoniums – green lime-scented *P.* 'Radula'; *P. capitatum* and *P. graveolens* both smelling like roses. Others chosen not only for scent but for delicacy, variegation, mysterious purply colour, oak-leaf shapes, hairy stems or an aerial form, were: *P. abrotanifolium, P. denticulatum, P. tetragonum, P. quercifolium*; 'Grey Lady Plymouth', 'Endsleigh', 'Prince of Orange', 'Paton's Unique' and 'Filicifolium' and so many others. Two of her geraniums whose leaves when crushed are overwhelmingly aromatic, were *G. macrorrhizum* (rock cranesbill), with deep crimson flowers, and the very spectacular *G. psilostemon* from Armenia, with vivid magenta flowers dramatized by black centres.

Violets, lilies and lavender; tobacco flowers, white and mauve fuchsias, oleanders and verbenas the colour of amethysts, were all greedily crammed in for their fragrance. Even sages, with their sweaty scent. And for the delicious evocation of vanilla and chocolate Anne Simonet placed her pots of heliotropes on a table at nose height. Against the walls were a honeysuckle, the common white jasmine, *Jasminum officinale*, and a fully double climbing rose, 'Clair Matin', smelling of sweet briar.

One plant with a particularly compliant life-style is *Solanum rantonnetii*. Though Madame Simonet primarily chose it for its fragrance in the cooler hours of the day, she explained with pleasure how the solanum, with its violet-blue flowers and small yellow eyes, keeps blooming for five months on end. An evergreen *Choisya ternata* with a scent of almonds, and a lightly fragrant *Abelia* x *grandiflora* with small leaves like pointed wings and miniature trumpet-shaped pink flowers, are two of Anne Simonet's beloved shrubs. Another plant which she loves because it is '*appréciable pour sa floraison tardive*', flowering well into October and early November, is an unusual shrub, *Podranea ricasoliana*, with weird bunches of two-inch funnel-shaped flowers, pink striped with red. 'Here we like autumn gardens because the countryside is very dry and we are without flowers from the beginning of August. And as it never freezes before December or January, it's completely possible to have a late garden.' Then she added, shrewdly, 'Well, as long as you are there throughout the summer.'

Large wooden tubs contained orange and lemon trees, but what really caught the eye were Madame Simonet's other containers. 'A small garden like this needs handsome pots,' she said, pointing to a glazed green one, traditional to Provence. Some of her pots were inexpensive, *des pots artisanaux*, hand-thrown and locally made, with scalloped edges. In one was a pretty geranium, 'Mrs Pollock', mottled like a crocodile; some were 'seconds' which she used upside-down as stands in crowded corners to gain height for certain plants she wanted to show to advantage, such as a *Convolvulus mauritanicus*, a plant I would give anything to grow for its twining grace and white-throated azure flowers. Other pots were *magnifiques* and extremely expensive, '*à cause de la Côte d'Azur*', Anne Simonet ruefully remarked. She bought them in Biot from the *poterie provençale de M. Augé Laribié*. Other superb pottery, decorated with lions' heads, garlands of flowers or bunches of grapes, came from Aubagne.

But whatever the pot, every one of them was of that soft terracotta colour so often found in the south of France, looking mellow and dusty as though covered with bloom. Not one was made of that aggressive red which curdles the colours in a garden. And in springtime how pretty they must look filled with pale rose tulips.

Among the white flowers, particularly cherished for their palpable fragrance, was a cistus, that large flowering aromatic one with dashes of spilt egg yolk at the base of each petal. This was *Cistus populifolius*, found so often among rocks, thickets and the *garrigue* of the Mediterranean. Dicentras, which I avoid for their colour of broken veins, are a totally different affair when white; *D. spectabilis* 'Alba', which Madame Simonet grows, has arching sprays of dangling flowers light as a feather. A white rose, which in England is usually the yellow variety, was the deliciously scented *Rosa banksiae* 'Alba plena', with long, twining thornless tendrils and small double flowers of immense charm. An early flowering evergreen was the susceptible *Loropetalum chinense*, with small flowers like white spiders clinging to the stems.

But most magnificent of all was her 'Angel's Trumpet'. *Datura suaveolens*, with heavy fragrance and white pendulous flowers, is truly '*une splendeur, très florifère et merveilleusement parfumée, mais très exigeante*' (very demanding), needing to be watered twice a day in hot weather and with an insatiable appetite for bonemeal and manure. It also needs to be brought inside in winter, and perhaps what is not so well known, the berries of the datura family are highly poisonous. According to Theophrastus – 372–287 BC, who in his old age gave up his study of plants to study his fellow-men – a minute portion of *Datura stramonium* and 'the patient becomes sportive and

A new part of Anne Simonet's courtyard garden.

thinks himself a fine fellow; twice this dose, the patient goes mad and has delusions', add a *soupçon* more and he becomes permanently insane, while an extra booster and it will be curtains.

One of Anne Simonet's regrets is that owing to the extreme heat of summer she cannot grow one of the older Hybrid Tea roses, 'Crimson Glory'. Her disappointment is not because of its deep velvety colour which fades to purple, but for its powerful perfume, which at dusk is overwhelming. Occasionally a tempest hurtles remorselessly through the hilltop village, eddying between the walls and leaving havoc in her courtyard from broken branches and parched earth. This is the *mistral*, the dry north-north-westerly which sweeps down from the Massif Central funnelling through the Rhône Valley and clearing the sky of clouds. Then there are the violent rainstorms, such as the one we had been driving through that day, which shatter the petals of her flowers in a few seconds. As she told us, they live on the edge of olive country, with the disadvantages of both the south and the north. '*Enfin, j'exagère un peu, mais c'est vrai que le jardin demande une attention extrême!*'

Growing plants for their scent is an indulgence in itself, but Madame Simonet has gone further. She has been collecting scented plants for five or six years. She asks people for sources, she takes cuttings and exchanges some of hers for those she needs. But always the great driving force, the lodestar which narrows her choice of plants, is not the confines of her small garden, but scent. 'I love smells. I've written on the smells of the *département*.' With the help of a colleague, she has produced what at first sight looks like a book, *Le Nez de la Drôme*, but open it up and instead of pages are twelve phials containing the essence of the Drôme: lavender, thyme, mint and lime flowers; peach, honey, olive oil and garlic; leather, truffles, *picadon* (a goat's cheese), and lastly cocoa which is used locally in the manufacture of chocolate. Each scent has an illustrated card with a brief outline of the product.

Anne Simonet has written about her own idiosyncratic sensitivity to smells; where a photographer would see a field of lavender bordered by broom as contrasts of grey-blue and yellow, Anne Simonet would smell the slightly crude and dry scent of lavender warming in the sun, with the sweeter, more rounded lower tones of broom. Our pleasurable or abhorrent reaction to smells is not inherent; our responses are conditioned. And she notes how we *craquons* (freak out) over the smell, say, of newly baked bread, whereas a Vietnamese would get high on the stench of fermented fish. We also find it difficult to recognize different scents. But why? Simply because we have been taught to read, to write, but never to smell.

She is leading us by the nose. With her collection of phials we pass through the Drôme from the fragile fragrance of flowers to the slightly denser scent of peaches; to *les effluves balsamiques des plantes aromatiques* (the balsamic fragrance of aromatic plants), to the powerful smell of garlic; and she even takes us underground for the almost animal scent of truffles. Finally, she persuades us to discover the equine smell of leather and the power of chocolate. Each scent is contained in her 'book' which she offers us as our first lesson on fragrance.

Yet that is not all. Anne Simonet takes us further. She goes on to write about the waning season when, as the year fades with the viney smell of the last grapes, there comes the first of the season's olive oil from around Nyons – *verte et parfumée* – a green smell barely touched with a *soupçon* of acidity. Winter is full of scent, she reminds us, and she writes eloquently about olive pressing in her region and vividly describes truffle hunting near Tricastin – the smell of rich humus, of mushrooms and of wet-coat-of-dog.

Cautiously she reveals a small part of the secret method for distilling her twelve essences but, she warns us, beware! One must have a good nose, of course, but olfactory saturation comes quickly! Too easily heightened sensitivity to smells can be temporarily blunted so that the wonderful journey of discovery is lost. Fortunately Tamsin and I stopped just in time. As we sat on her terrace surrounded by pots of scented plants, trying at the same time to identify each little flask as it was offered to us, our senses had almost become impervious.

Although she was expecting her baby to be born that week, Anne Simonet was already making further plans for the garden. She was going to extend it to an upper terrace, to '*mon futur jardin*' she explained as we stood up there looking over the encircling walls towards the Ardèche. Naturally she will fill the place with plants smelling of spices and fruit, of incense and resins, of honey, musk or animals. And when even she has reached satiety, from this hill-top terrace she will be able to sit and look out over her flowers to a very different horizon.

On the overcast day we were there it was hard to make out the distant hills. But I can imagine how, when the air is clear, her eye will skim over the intervening industry and see a sweep of unspoilt country where the river Ardèche cuts through gorges and where, at certain times of the year, a wall of converging water, formidable and impressive, advances towards the Rhône at the speed of nine to twelve miles an hour. Almost within touching distance, Anne Simonet can move from her revived lime tree, her flowery enclosure, her phials of distilled scents, to a grandeur and ferocity of landscape on a leviathan scale.

COLD WINDS WITH SALT
THAT BURNS

On an island off the coast of Brittany, where the boat is met by a cart drawn by a tractor named *Le Vieux Trainard*, we came to see a garden. The owner, encased from head to foot in yellow oilskins, was waiting on the quayside in a deluge of squally cloudbursts. A garden in this weather? We were reckless. But the trouble with our kind of intense garden quest is that we cannot allow for any slack; we make appointments which may be miles apart but which have to fit in with the gardeners' own lives – perhaps with their weekends in the country, the only time we can find them at home. And compared with our own small congested island, France is a vast territory to traverse, where many hours are squandered crossing from one *département* to another.

The *Association des Parcs Botaniques de France* may sound a formidable title, a bit intimidating, a bit po-faced, but it is through its members that we found gardens of very personal distinction. Madame Maryvonne Sentuc is one of their most distinguished members.

On our crossing to the island, crushed among a plethora of wet shopping, trickling hair and crackling plastic macs as we huddled with tourists and islanders in the tiny cabin to avoid the tempest outside, I felt somewhat inadequate. Some botanists can be very earnest. A close friend, whose passion is searching for wild flowers and who describes the position she takes up when on the campaign as 'bottomizing', is a rare species; laughter and plant identification are not usually instinctive partners. Coming to meet Maryvonne Sentuc I was prepared to be overwhelmed with nomenclature and science; I assumed that a studious and knowing demeanour would be expected and that I should be totally out of my depth. Dear Madame Sentuc – generous and gentle, and without a trace of horticultural solemnity.

As we were drying ourselves out in front of her bright fire, in spite of it being the first week of June, and having tea and little strawberry tarts, Maryvonne Sentuc began to tell us about herself. 'This is an extraordinary house – because it is the house of my dreams!' She spoke with such sparkling enthusiasm that all my preconceptions of what an APBF member

Madame Sentuc's concern is for a garden not in conflict with the sea.

would be like, fell away. 'I knew this house as a very small girl. I used to pick the snails out of the walls with my fingers whenever I passed by!'

Love for the place had, for generations, become deeply fused into the fibre of her family. Her father, a doctor, adored the island; he had spent his childhood here, so when he had his own family he brought them here for their holidays. 'It had a lot of charm then because there were no tourists. There were only four or five families and no ugly constructions. Already we find the port with its souvenir shops appalling. Then in summer we're invaded by tourists who leave paper everywhere.' She spoke with compassion, not anger. 'But the island has to live. It's a poor island, there are no factories, no resources – nothing. The *mairie* has two men who work on the roads. Not enough money to pay more.'

When Monsieur and Madame Sentuc brought their own small children to visit the island they were the fifth generation to become bewitched by the enchanted atmosphere. In 1977 they came to look for a house, and found that this eighteenth-century one – the house of her dreams – was owned by a lawyer from Rennes, who had lived here for years before abandoning it; yet unfortunately the house was not for sale. Instead, they bought another one, further from the harbour, where they could come for holidays.

Ten years passed before the stars in Maryvonne Sentuc's firmament shifted; the property came up for sale, and she knew that there had always been an incontrovertible destiny linking her to the house since childhood. But how was she to inveigle her husband? 'Oh, it's such a lovely house!' How to convince him that they should at least look at it? 'Near the port – with a view over the sea and yet so sheltered.' The answer she got was not unexpected: 'There's no question of it,' her husband said, 'we have a house, we can't move.'

Two months later they came to see it. '*C'est très bien!*' her husband cautiously admitted. 'For me,' declared Madame Sentuc emphatically, 'it was magic! Absolute magic.' She turned towards the window. 'Oh, the light over the sea – it was so beautiful.' Ruefully she added, 'And it was expensive. We sold the other house, and then, *enfin*, we bought this! That's what we did.' Her impetuosity, her unshakeable belief that the house and land had always been moving inexorably towards her, was summed up in two words: 'Absolutely mad!'

Neglected, the place had been asleep for years. The strong walls were intact, the foundations were sound, and the beautiful grey tiled roof was rain-proof. When we walked indoors, it felt like putting on a coat already well warmed by its owner; a garment that fitted and was comforting. The dining room had low ceilings, a dresser with nineteenth-century faience plates called '*barbotuie*' decorated with pink, blue and yellow flowers and green leaves, and country furniture including one of those huge handsome French *armoires*, which now have become so fashionable and expensive abroad, which Madame Sentuc had stripped of its brown varnish so that it looked like handled satin. Colours were sleepy, unobtrusive; they did nothing to detract from the view outside.

Through a kitchen window Maryvonne Sentuc and I peered at a nearby wall and a self-clinging *Pileostegia viburnoides* with narrow leathery leaves, and creamy flowers to reflect the light. 'Next to them is an acacia so that the yellow and white brighten my outlook.' The land had been neglected for years, but for Maryvonne Sentuc, who belongs to that growing breed of passionate gardeners, total dereliction did nothing to quench her perseverance. Speaking about her indecisions when she first started and of the vagaries of the weather, she said, 'I like to be enclosed, I need protection – but I like open spaces – though great expanses do distress me a little.' And then she spoke of her perpetual dilemma: 'The difficulty is I have the sea! I don't want to shut out the view, nor do I want a garden in conflict with it. How difficult! I want harmony, the colours to remain gentle – not violent colours.' Although Maryvonne Sentuc was apologetic about the weather, I thought the sullen light enhanced the colours. The blues, mauves and pinks seemed almost to quicken under the reeking damp.

While Tamsin and Cassandra stayed within the shelter of the house, Madame Sentuc and I walked through her garden under alternating scuds of violent rain and scraps of sunlight. At the entrance to her house she had planted two Irish yews. 'One mustn't plant too many flowers round or up the house, one must leave it *sévère* because it's so handsome as it is.' The earth around the house is impoverished and windswept; lower down, where there was once a *potager*, the soil is shallow, sandy and dry. '*Quand même*, it's good for cistus and thyme! But rhododendrons – which I adore – I knew it was no use!' Maryvonne Sentuc's approach to planting is cerebral. She would buy one plant, 'And if she's happy, I buy more. There's no point in forcing it . . . but if I see a plant that's happy – well, from that moment I start a collection because it means the climate suits it and I can have all the varieties of that one particular plant.'

On a small terrace made of slate, looking as black as charcoal in the rain, was a summer-house. Doors the blue of scabious led inside where the floor was paved with blue stone as old as the house; there were white cane chairs covered with bluey-green cotton faded to the colour of the sea on cloudy days. From here Maryvonne Sentuc could contemplate her garden with an appraising eye. Gardens seen with a bird's eye view are impressive; you become immediately aware of a different latitude. Her paths, made from stones bought in Alsace for their colour of '*vieux rose*', were enhanced by the dry stone walls and were sharpened by vivid patches of moss.

Maryvonne Sentuc not only has this elevated outlook from the summer-house onto paths where prostrate rosemary and salvias like velvet have tousled up the edges – beyond she has the sea. There are no words graphic enough to describe the effect of this view as a background to a garden. Coloured boats dip at anchor in the harbour, gulls continually glide and swoop, their wings making white smears against the sulky sky and the dimly visible mainland, and over the sea a mist causes small waves to make steely reflections across the surface of the water. Words failed. The only response was an inarticulate ah-h-h . . .

'We started with the garden down here. It was high with nettles and bindweed – the nightmare of gardeners – and there we discovered the trace of a kind of cross design with a well in the centre. I kept that shape – it was odd. It's such an old well.' So close to sea level, the water is brackish but usable. Years ago the women used to draw the water from the well for washing their clothes and for cleaning fish. Within the four triangles, which are not symmetrically planted, are heathers, abutilons, fennels and rock roses, including *Cistus ladanifer* with white petals smeared with coffee in the centre, and another, *C. populifolius*, stained with yellow. Twice a year Madame Sentuc crops the milky-green leaves of *Cistus* x *corbariensis*, whose crimson buds open into mounded cushions of papery white flowers. 'They are so *mignons! Très adorables!*' she exclaimed with fervour. Here too is a spectacular shrub, *Ozothamnus rosmarinifolius*, with red buds opening into white flowers, and a winter-flowering *Daphne mezereum* smelling of summer. Twining plants such as a *Stauntonia hexaphylla* with chocolate-scented white flowers tinged with purple, a high-flying white clematis, *C. indivisa*, and a densely scented, self-clinging *Trachelospermum asiaticum*, merge and flow with abundant luxuriance.

Some of the shrubby plants are cut into the ornamental spheres which are so prevalent and pretty in France; others of reliable fortitude can be placed wherever Maryvonne Sentuc pleases. A hebe, for instance, 'Great Orme', with spikes of pink flowers, is a staunch survivor in saline breezes and even has a second flowering at the end of the summer; the fragrant *Olearia paniculata*, renowned as a maritime stalwart, has wavy, acid-green leaves and humble flower-heads with a scent in October brought by the evening sea breeze. '*Quel parfum vous arrive le soir, avec la brise de la mer!*'

With other plants she has to be careful, by making use of levels and

Here the village women used to come to wash their clothes and clean the fish.

walls, to protect the flowers from salt winds. Escallonias, tree mallows and those consummate flowers, romneya, white as snow, filled with yellow stamens and with silvery-grey crenellated leaves, are herded into the sanctuary of walls. The weird *Corokia cotoneaster*, descriptively known as the 'Wire-netting Bush' for its tortuous tracery of twigs and dark green leaves, white-felted beneath, is praised by Maryvonne Sentuc for its starry yellow flowers and orange fruit seen glowing against the walls. The showy *Euphorbia characias* is a spurge with heads of clustering flowers of vibrant lime green. 'I love it for its magnificence, its vigour, beauty and the way it goes so superbly with the blue of echiums' – in particular her *Echium fastuosum*, with flowers like sumptuous blue candles.

The garden is full of unexpected steps and corners and bits of historical legacies left over from a time when sheep and fishing were part of the life-style of the island. A little building which had once been a *bergerie* – a sheepfold – stands on her land; another secret retreat has two white benches and two ancient walnuts, trees which in spring have leaves the colour of bruised peaches and a smell so biting when the leaves are crushed that it penetrates to the top of the skull.

In October of 1987 disaster struck. Twenty tall pines were destroyed in a

hurricane. 'They were ancient trees, they were beautiful trees and I cried
and cried because . . . I know I shall never see them again.' And the climate
usually? 'It's very gentle. The coldest here was minus five, but we never
have bitter weather for more than two or three days. What we do have are
strong winds. Cold ones with salt which burns.' Even so plants from
southern France do well, such as mimosa, cistus and lavenders; so too do
pittosporums and trails of *Convolvulus mauritanicus*, but to her great regret
magnolias shrivel and die in the face of the ferocity of that wind. There are
none on the island. Camellias, too, barely make it.

What Madame Sentuc does grow, in great abundant blue masses because
they do so well for her, are ceanothus. 'I would like to have a complete
collection.' Among them is the small, rather sticky-leaved *C*. x *mendo-
cinensis*, with flowers the blue of Wedgwood china; the rather misleadingly
named *C. delineanus* 'Topaz', a light indigo blue; 'Italian Skies' with cobalt
flowers; and *C. arboreus* 'Trewithen Blue' of such impeccable azure blue
that, when it is in full flower, its ravishing intensity overwhelms
everything within sight.

The silvery leaves and pink buds of *Convolvulus cneorum* are everywhere.
As Maryvonne Sentuc said, it is '*tellement heureux chez moi*'. It does so well
with her that she has to cut it back as though she were dealing with tough,
springy box. Correas, named after an eighteenth-century Portuguese
botanist, are fine evergreens from the antipodes. Here the *C. backhouseana* is
a tall plant with dangling greeny-white flowers which blend well with
plants of a more pushy countenance. Madame Sentuc is devoted to an
unusual North American shrub, *Holodiscus discolor*. It produces clouds of
flowers like a lather of creamy froth, which again makes a good foil for
anything with a spirited deportment. Pointing enthusiastically to a
sarcococca, with its underpowered floral output but musky scent after rain
which makes up for any visual shortcomings, she exclaimed, '*C'est
merveilleux. Je l'adore.*' And as for her *Azara microphylla*, that most elegant
of evergreens, with yellow flowers smelling of vanilla, she almost hummed
with delight.

'I love rocks, but . . . it's only that I can't stand making rockeries,' she
said as we walked beyond the garden to the wild land that slopes down to
where the stones of her walls imperceptibly weld into the rocks of the coast
and where agapanthus, which grow everywhere in gardens on the island,
are freely given their blue heads to flow along the margin of the sea. Before
the catastrophic felling of the pine trees there was not a house in sight; now
she has had to become reconciled. She sighed with the inevitability that
overcomes all gardeners faced with calamities. Like them she makes new

plans. '*Voilà – c'est comme ça.*' She indicated the walls on the edge of her garden. 'Now my idea is . . . you understand – those lovely walls – I want to continue them in yew. Perhaps it'll work.' She raised her arms to indicate height. 'Then, here in the hedge, I'll make a round hole so that turning around one will have a view.' I felt a lurch of warm-hearted compatibility when I heard her say that. For so long I have wondered why people who have a dazzling view do not begin, immediately, by hiding it. They could then contrive to let the view appear in glimpses, so that anticipation would be heightened and the impact would be sensational.

As we walked back towards the welcome shelter of the house Maryvonne Sentuc said, 'I do so like clematis with trees. And I want lots more ceanothus and white broom.' Then she added as an explanation, 'It's not so much flowers I like – I love shrubs! One has to put in flowers, *enfin* – but not too many. They create so much maintenance. Look – this is lovely, isn't it? It's a grevillea, and this is a little *Drimys aromatica.*'

We stood for a moment while she looked critically at some of her beds. 'I find English gardeners marvellous because they know how to mix colours. They are the architects of the countryside. They don't impose flowers which don't suit the location. Here,' and she looked towards her beautiful, sensitive and incomparable garden, 'it's raw! I suppose it's the sea.' Then with that cool philosophy which I was to come across often among French gardeners, she added, 'Yet if there are imperfections – *tant pis!*'

Like so many gardens, though by no means all, Madame Sentuc's is completely personal to her. It is as intimate and reflective of her personality as the garden belonging to Catherine Vercken in the Côte d'Or. Not only does Maryvonne Sentuc do all the work herself, but her strong feelings for the house, beloved since childhood, have become part of her commitment to the garden. 'This is a thing one does . . .' She paused. 'I say that it is a present for the children – I have three sons and a daughter – and I think my daughter likes the garden, but not in the same way as myself.' She stood looking out towards the scudding clouds, 'I can't make a painting, but . . . I can plant a tree.'

Wherever you walk through the garden there is an awareness of the sea; the smell of wrack, the scream of sea birds and a heightened perception that at any moment the brutality of the elements, unseen but potential, could change a benign day into chaos. Leaving her, crossing back to the mainland in a choppy sea, we could see her diminishing figure waving to us from the pier. And I remembered her bleak words which are at the heart of gardening: 'One thing is certain – that when one disappears – that day the garden will be over.'

Some Irrepressible Gardeners

'BAH – YOU'D HAVE
NO POTATOES!'

If there is one part of France which evokes an instant picture of what that country means, it must be Burgundy. It is not that I know the region better than anywhere else, nor that I love Burgundy above all other places, but just that it is redolent of everything French. Maybe it is the agriculture, maybe it is the churches or small towns, or perhaps it is just good meals and a sense of well-being.

Years ago, before there were autoroutes, and when in the 'fifties we were allowed to travel, my husband Michael and I often took the ferry to the down-at-heel port of Dunkerque (but to our eyes a town shimmering with beauty), and made our leisurely journey through places seldom spoken of today with such sonorous names as Hazebrouck, Béthune, Bapaume and Peronne. Everywhere we were slowed down by the bone-shaking *pavé*, the cobbles circling the periphery of each town for a few kilometres beyond its boundaries. It was a time when in every village there were ancient pumps worked by hand or else a spring of flowing water where we could replenish our drinking bottles or the radiator of the car, and where women came to fill their buckets. It was a time, too, when as a matter of course double beds in hotels were sagging ditches, private baths were unheard of and when the lavatories were often holes in the floor with perilous foot-rests and erratic water.

France! – heady, exciting; with an involuntary quickening of our spirits we would stop in some town square when parking was easy, theft unheard of, and look for the Café de Commerce for our first taste of real coffee served in bowls with ears, and a place where every meal was considered inadequate unless accompanied by a green salad.

But not until we reached the southern margins of the great champagne country around the city of Troyes, which we always mispronounced, did we feel we were on the threshold of authentic France. I do not understand what made us ache for a country that was not our own, for a country we hardly knew then and yet which we instinctively responded to without a trace of rational judgement or academic reasoning. France was French, and that in itself made us notch up our responses in a way not even Italy could

PREVIOUS PAGE
A small concession to space among the roses in André Eve's garden.

do, for all its immediate sensualities. And now, years later, after motoring thousands of miles through the country, the word Burgundy still gives me a pang of anticipation.

We were travelling towards a kitchen garden right in the heartland of France, in the southern fringes of Burgundy near the Romanesque church of Tournus and the abbey of Cluny. Near, too, Milly-Lamartine. About twelve years ago Michael and I came to the village of Milly looking for nostalgia: looking for the place where Lamartine, the greatest Burgundian poet, wrote his evocative poems of childhood, and where he used to return to sleep, imagining he heard still 'the voice of my mother when I wake up, the footsteps of my father, and my sisters' happy cries . . .'. We peered through the iron gates of his family house, closely shuttered and sadly deserted; we looked at the bronze bust of the poet on a hideous pedestal in front of the *mairie*, and thought of his words: '. . . the sweet and melancholy voices of the little frogs that sing on summer evenings'.

Now I was back with my daughter and granddaughter a few miles from Milly, looking for the *potager* of the feudal château of Berzé-le-Chatel high on a hill dominating the southern approaches to Cluny. We had made no assignation, we had no contact, but by blundering in and stating the reason for our intrusion we found a gardener who could not have been more helpful or more mercurial.

Joaquim da Costa, a Portuguese, has very green eyes. He is also articulate and funny and without doubt knows his onions. In fact, flowers do not interest him. 'All the flowers! *Bah*. For myself I'm not so keen on flowers. Who says the gardens of Holland are beautiful with so many flowers?' He paused, threw out his hands, and announced 'Me? I adore everything that is vegetable!'

We were standing just inside the great gateway at the end of an avenue of trees which leads to the château belonging to the Comte and Comtesse de Milly. Five round defensive towers of ochre stone remain; once there were seven, until part of the château was destroyed in the Revolution. On our left were steps covered with pots of flowers (presumably tended by Madame da Costa) leading to the gatehouse where Joaquim and his wife live.

Twenty-two years ago Joaquim, who was then twenty-four, brought his seventeen-year-old wife to France. Now their daughter is a medical student at Bourg-en-Bresse, their son is at college, and until last year when the old comte and his wife died, well into their eighties, Joaquim's wife was the cook at the château and Joaquim was employed wearing different hats – at times he was the butler, at others he served at table, and sometimes he put on the chauffeur's cap. Gesturing towards the château he exclaimed, 'In there I was unhappy. All day long wearing a white shirt, a bow tie – and when I went out – the *casquette*! Opening car doors! . . . I did it all. But I didn't like it!' In the past year his life has been turned inside out. Literally. The present comte, with whom he gets on very well, has given him the freedom of the gardens and, more significantly, of the *potager*.

With spontaneous intimacy, as though he was revealing a secret aberration, Joaquim said, 'You know, *j'adore la nature*. I love my work now. The garden! But what I love is nature – and hunting. Not for the pleasure of killing. When I go hunting my wife says, "How is it that the neighbour kills two or three hares and you only kill one in a season?" But my taste is not for killing – my taste is for going out with my dog. To look at the countryside, the trees.' And he turned towards the view of placid scenery and admitted, 'Sometimes, you know, *je suis capable de passer une journée après une sauterelle!*' – of spending a day watching a grasshopper, or a grass snake. 'I watch them, but leave them. If I see a rabbit or hare – I don't shoot – I can't! I walk by.'

While we moved slowly towards the château Joaquim kept up a steady flow of information. On the estate there were four hundred and fifty hectares of rich meadowland, one hundred and fifty hectares of woodland and seven hectares of vines. Until recently there had been a gardener who had worked on the estate for forty-five years. 'He was a very old man. I got on so well with him because there at the house there wasn't much to do after the mealtimes were over, so I passed time with him. I liked him very much.'

Now that he has a free hand Joaquim keeps chickens and rabbits; he can plant vegetables, or lay down grass if he prefers. The present comte, who lives in Paris, visits infrequently, apart from the summer when he comes with his family for three months. They have *l'esprit parisien*, is how Joaquim put it, and as long as he maintains the château and attends to the upkeep, he is left alone. (On a second visit to the castle, I did meet the comte. He spoke warmly of Joaquim, telling me how much he depended on him, not only as the caretaker but how willingly he would cope with disasters, such as when most of the roof blew off.)

Joaquim led us first to the top terrace under the high windows of the château so that we could get the best view of the kitchen garden and see its design laid out, a long way below us, on the bottom terrace. Small oval beds were outlined in low box and contained fruit trees which are now unobtainable; neither their pears nor their apples are to be found any longer in the markets. Iris and phlox grew under the trees, but apart from the

The chemin de ronde *dividing the potager from the hills of Burgundy.*

throbbing crimson of peonies everything else was small and potential. By late June the whole effect would have changed.

As we walked round the end of the château, passing beautiful long farm buildings on our way to the *potager*, Joaquim answered our questions with unflagging verve: 'It's so good to have one's own produce!' he said dancing about in front of us. 'To have salad in the garden! Tomatoes! Haricot beans! I do it all!' He told us how he liked to follow the old traditions; how he loved to think that the garden had kept the same form for more than fifty years. Only the plantings of vegetables change each year as he rotates the crops. 'Each has its own way of using the soil. If you kept them always in one place – *bah*, you'd have no potatoes!'

The kitchen garden was held within the embrace of low walls seeded with little ferns and stonecrop and overlooking the huge head of an acacia dense with creamy flowers that stood on a grassy slope far below; beyond was pastoral landscape with higgledy-piggledy fields, pastures glazed with yellow buttercups, willows and white cows. The day was still; occasionally there was the strident sound of a cock crowing cutting through the distant sound of birdsong. It was easy to imagine how this outlook had remained generation after generation without a trace of industry or a sight of those huge farm hangars which blemish so much of the countryside here and in Britain. 'There's been a *potager* as long as the château has existed,' Joaquim told us. 'Soil was brought in to make the garden. See, there's a *chemin de ronde*.' The circuit is a precarious path running along the top of the wall, where at one point there is a small gazebo built out of the wall with hoops of iron holding up the sagging heads of a sumptuous wisteria. Did Joaquim sit there? 'No, but look, I made a tunnel of virginia creeper where I sometimes come to sit.' So too does his daughter. 'She dreams a lot – even too much. She comes here with a bag of books.' He turned to us for agreement. 'One must be mad to study medicine! She knows how to stick the needle in, even in the dark – but to cook a carrot . . . *Bah!*'

Joaquim's kitchen garden is not meticulous. Being Portuguese, he has no inbuilt French tendency compelling him towards order. Its charm lies in a certain arbitrary dishevelment in which blackcurrant bushes seem to have restlessly wandered here and there. ('Apart from blackcurrant syrup, *cassis*, we don't use them.') His raspberries, strawberries and gooseberries are more restrained. Rows of potatoes, following the curve of the terrace, cross lines of garlic and onions, red and green lettuces, batavia, 'red carrots' and tomatoes already staked out. Radishes, thyme, dusky purple sages, chives and parsley are interspersed with small handfuls of asters, gladioli and sweet peas, along with the prescribed slab of soil prepared for the dahlias.

'I have oleanders, too,' he told us as we stood under the ramparts where a rose, the mauve-pink of stormy clouds at sunset, climbed unhindered up the high walls. He took up a pick, worn shiny with use and with a handle as glossy as satin. 'But they are a lot of work.' In winter he brings the oleanders indoors for four months. Then, jabbing at the earth with the pick, he added as an afterthought, 'You know, they just grow along the roads in Portugal.' And does he go back there? 'Not often. *La France – c'est un pays merveilleux*! I realized immediately that the people are good.' Occasionally he visits Portugal to see his family when he has money, but feels no pain at the separation.

One year he went to visit the châteaux of the Loire. 'I saw other *potagers* there. Yes! More beautiful than this, but made for the eye only. There was one – I don't remember which one it was . . . oh, *merde*, what *is* the name of the château . . . ? Well anyway there were long rows with terraces, with beautiful gardens beneath – with a row of leeks, one of lettuces, one of beetroot, one of cabbage, one of haricots, and each tomato plant the same height. Row after row, all beautifully ordered and aligned.' Then with a shrug and grimace of dismissal he added, 'There wasn't a blade of grass, a weed . . . there was nothing! *Ce n'est pas la même chose! Voilà* – this one is *un jardin d'exploitation*. A garden that is used! From which one benefits!' And then with a final ebulliant justification: 'Which one eats!'

We had now reached the far end of the garden where it curves round the ramparts, and suddenly we were into an almost tangible scent, dense and overwhelming, from a massive philadelphus which grew beside the entrance to a tower. Pushing open the door Joaquim led us into the cool gloom, with the damp smell of earth mixed with the homely smell of sawn logs stacked in tiers and the astringency of garlic. 'Here is where I put the onions and garlic – on that platform – too high for rats to climb and it never freezes. It's perfect for fruit too.' Then with barely a break in intonation he added, 'And it's here where they shut up a man and a bullock.' Our bewilderment must have been apparent. 'Yes, yes! And they shut the doors on them to see which would survive the longest. Well . . . it was the man who died first. The animal two days later – because it licked the walls which contain saltpetre.' Who did this? He looked at us as if it was a silly question. '*Eh bien, les rois de France, madame*!' Yes, of course. Naturally. But what about the goodness of the French you were speaking about? 'Ah, they are now good, today, *quand même*. But French history is horrible! When one speaks of Napoléon . . . well, *Napoléon, c'est un salopard*! All the French love him! But, you know . . .' Joaquim continued opening his eyes expressively so that we would understand the full horror of his next words,

'He went as far as Portugal to invade!'

We moved on into what had once been the chapel, built right into the foundations of the château. Under the domed roof Joaquim showed us his collection of old gardening tools. They were not museum pieces, but spades, hoes and rakes he still uses. He picked up a well-worn mattock and shook it. 'See! The handle is like the teeth of my grandmother!' Here too his beetroots and carrots were bedded down in sand. He pulled out a carrot, wiped it cursorily on his sleeve and ate it. 'See! It's too cold here for courgettes and aubergines – and once I even tried three or four peppers.'

Outside, built against the wall, was a magnificent and very old greenhouse. The kind made with small panes of glass surrounded by slender fillets of wood. Inside he sows seeds; he has grown a lemon tree he brought from Portugal, and a banana tree which never fruits. 'I have to buy bananas and then hang them on the tree when I want the real thing!' He showed us pile upon pile of very old, tiny earthenware pots used for seedlings. 'The plastic ones are useless – they break. And look at the difference. Here are geraniums in the old earthenware, and these, not doing so well, in plastic!'

Walking through the herb garden he told us how everything his wife knows about cooking she learned in France. 'She adores cooking! She is very good at cooking for the *noblesse française*, but as for aromatic dishes or recipes of the south of France . . .' he threw up his hands in despair, 'Zero! She knows me. I like the spicy, piquant dishes of Portugal – but she only knows French cuisine.' He pinched off a piece of herb and handed it to Tamsin to test her knowledge, and when she told him it was tarragon, he waved his arms with delight. 'You see! My daughter wouldn't care, and I do love a branch of tarragon in the middle of a roast chicken, it gives a wonderful taste! But tarragon doesn't grow easily in France, so what I do is put rabbit droppings underneath, and when I cut it back for winter I put more on top – to stop it freezing.' How lovely. I have always been enchanted to think how liquid manure turns into a peach; now, what wonder! rabbit droppings which mutate into tarragon.

Before we left, Joaquim took us to see his topiary. In the courtyard in front of the château there are seven large box trees rather like chess pawns. They were planted in 1894 and one of his jobs is to maintain their impeccable symmetry. 'This is a French garden,' he said with pride, pointing to the segments of lawn surrounded by low box hedges which had been laid out in 1911 by the present comte's grandfather. 'A real French garden of the nobility.' And then, with a mischievous glint in his green eyes, he added, 'There are no flowers!'

Joaquim's greenhouse, squatting under the walls of the château,
where he grows his fruitless banana tree.

SHE SAID IT USED TO
BE A SAD PLACE

'*Tout le monde fleurit son jardin!*' said Madame Arlette rolling her r's extravagantly. She was describing her origins around the river Orne in Normandy, in an area known as *la Suisse Normande* because of its escarpments, wooded valleys and occasional peaks, and for its rocks and dramatic gorges. And where, according to Arlette Malgras, everyone grew flowers. This explained it. We had drifted by sheer chance into the courtyard of her hotel. A courtyard absolutely sizzling with fervid colours.

We had come because of the nearby Courson Flower Show. Accommodation was almost impossible to find, with Germans, Dutch, Belgians as well as French horticultural enthusiasts filling any available space. Some instinct of Tamsin's had led us to the Hostellerie de St-Caprais, with only five bedrooms, located about six miles from Courson, in the village of St Vrain, and the courtyard, as we entered under the arched entrance, bowled us over with throbbing floral discord. But what utter enchantment to find hidden in the unprepossessing territory which lies amid the urban sprawl between Paris and Étampes. Any disgruntlement we had felt in making such a long journey from the south-west where we had been visiting a garden, was dispelled immediately.

Until twelve years ago Arlette Malgras had worked in a bank and her husband in a restaurant in Paris. The property they bought at St Vrain, a village of over two thousand inhabitants, consisted originally of two houses. From these they have made a large restaurant, with just a few hotel bedrooms. 'We didn't want it to look too much like a restaurant, you see. We wished to preserve the character of the place and the style of an old house.' They have succeeded. From the outside the hotel looks unpretentious; it lacks any of those ugly modern additions which have wrecked so many good, old inns, covered in Virginia creeper, which used to be so prevalent in France. 'I find it more *agréable* like this, don't you think?' Arlette spoke fast, with great eagerness; she was small and blonde and darted about from the kitchen to reception, from the dining-room to the garden.

She and her husband had made the garden out of a cobbled courtyard. 'There was nothing before – in fact it was a sad place!' Arlette cried waving her arms at our surroundings. It was hard to believe now; dolefulness had been banished, not a shadow of sobriety remained. As we sat having lunch in a galaxy of simmering colours – scarlet, magenta and carmine, livid purple, orange, chrome and ultramarine – Arlette told us how they had begun by laying down the small grass lawns, very neat, and very vivid, before making the first flower-bed. 'My husband designs and I have *la main verte.*' The result was a knock-out. Geraniums, petunias, campanulas, roses, and pink, button-shaped daisies, miniature pine trees, laurels, conifers and a weeping birch surrounded four round dining tables with pink tablecloths standing under striped umbrellas. Pansies swarmed; their royal petals, yellow and velvety purple, filled the foreground where golden conifers were backed against the walls. Ivy, used as ground-cover, formed a sober background to lobelias, fuchsias and explosive begonias. Eating lunch in such a setting requires robust health and good eyesight. The first throb of a migraine and you will totter yearningly towards the dark.

In the centre of the garden was a very large pot held together by strands of wire. Its green glaze, streaked with yellow, was crazed by old age, and earthenware showed through small chipped blemishes. 'The pot was here when we arrived, when we bought the house, and I kept it because I adore it! Look!' We did. It was jammed with puce geraniums. 'I love old things! I adore browsing in antique shops. I've furnished the children's rooms with old furniture because it gives me pleasure. I buy bits of furniture for when we leave this place. For when we retire. *J'ai des coups de coeur comme ça.*' Blows to her heart, as she so vividly described it. 'Look! That *sapin*, see how it's grown – like my children!' She smiled with warmth. 'I get on well with my youngest – especially well. It's unusual, isn't it, for a boy of twenty to talk to his mother? We have the same taste, though. Oh my! What a party we gave for his twentieth. A surprise! Seventy young friends and enough champagne . . !'

Arlette's zest was unquenchable. Her passion for the small garden gushed like a hot geyser. So too did her enthusiasm for old pots and stones. She would never compromise by using plastic. Polystyrene classical urns would have been an outrage. 'I try to find pots that are old-looking – rustic, country pots. I find it's better like that!' Old stones from the cellar steps had been brought up into the daylight to be used as steps and paving. She threw out her hands effusively, '*Bof!*' I prefer them to cement slabs.'

At the end of the courtyard furthest from the restaurant was a large raised terrace with steps leading up to it. Here the sun beat relentlessly against the high wall of the neighbouring building, reflecting back from the stone floor so that the area was a continual dilemma to Arlette. 'Palm trees

– I lost three or four there on the terrace. It was too hot. It absorbs the heat. I once had a large oriental vase there, very pretty with big plants, but they all got burnt. It grilled them.' I suggested rather mundanely that perhaps overhead vines would make an expansive green shaded area for her pots, but she had her sights fixed on something far more theatrical. A fountain. 'A big fountain in the middle! I've been looking in the antique shops for an old cast-iron one.' Her eyes sparkled. 'With a gargoyle and with the flowing water! What freshness! My husband's told me he could do that for me . . . so, *enfin*, it's possible.'

Her husband, between bouts of cooking, was as keen to construct things as Arlette was to fill every space with flowers. 'You see the pool there? My husband made it. We went to find the stones in the country, in a quarry, and he built all that.' The pool was full of brown, beige, gold and blue fish gliding, twisting and catching the light in sudden flashes of fluorescence. They were not for eating but for decoration, though occasionally predatory musk rats did invade the pool which meant an excursion had to be made to find replacements. On one side of the lawn was a natural underground spring which made sporadic gushing noises as it rose to the surface, filling the pool with fresh water and the courtyard with the soothing sound of rainfall.

Morning and evening Arlette was out among her flowers, petting and tending them with fanatical devotion. 'Oh, the garden is very beautiful at the end of July, the beginning of August! See over there. I've just pricked out the impatiens. They make a really pretty flower-bed – there beyond the red geraniums. And later there'll be dahlias too! I'll show you some photographs.' She prinked at a cushion of intensely blue campanulas like a hairdresser over an exquisite *coiffure*, and then with almost the same gesture tweaked the cheek of Cassandra who was sitting on the grass. '*Tu es une petite coquine*!' she said with endearing good humour.

After twenty-four hours staying in this heavenly place, we had come to terms with Madame's priorities. We began to understand. For miles around people came to the hotel for their anniversaries, christenings, business presentations and for weddings – *les noces*. Bookings were continually being made weeks in advance and it was easy to understand why. Monsieur Malgras's cooking was fine, but the floral arrangements were irresistible. Naturally, under those circumstances, comfort in the bedrooms was irrelevant. Arlette Malgras was not to be deflected – though at first we tried.

We had been supplied with a leather-bound edition of the complete works of Molière, and a white bust of Beethoven standing on a tiny table

A more restrained corner of the explosive planting at St Vrain.

just inside the bedroom door, and the lack of a bathroom shelf was irrelevant because there was no tooth glass; towels had to lie across the lavatory cistern, and there was no plug to the wash basin. 'Try the bath plug,' Arlette amiably suggested. We had, we told her, and it was too big. 'Tomorrow I'll buy one.' But it never came. A bulb for the bedside light? A pillow? *'D'accord, d'accord,'* came her placatory promises. They never appeared, naturally; Arlette Malgras's heart was elsewhere. Plumbing and light bulbs were trivia to someone who had her sights set on filling every pot and vase with high-pitched flowers whose colour decibels reached visual dissonance.

These arrived each morning from the florist. 'Every day I do about twenty or thirty vases for the house. It's a lot of work, but I love it. I'd like to buy masses of flowers!' Looking around I thought she had already reached the Plimsoll line. 'Masses of plants, masses and masses! But we are limited for space – so I have them in the house!' You might think she was talking of discreet little posies for each dining-table, but she was not. Her vases were filled with dynamic explosions of hi-tech ingenuity. Intemperate striped lilies of outrageous vulgarity, mind-numbing roses of cerise edged with apricot; rose-buds of such corrosive orange you hoped you would have left the hotel before they opened. There were flaming gladioli which periodically let off steam, and carnations whose rioting colours would cause an uprising in a graveyard. Yet it required only a slight mental readjustment to achieve a different attitude of mind to all this turbulence. The vases, the garden, were magnificent.

Here, in the courtyard at St Vrain, Arlette's garden had reached visual amplitude. What, therefore, were a few shortcomings in the bedrooms compared with what was pulsating downstairs? I would go again to the hotel at the drop of a hat for the joy of sharing her extravagant delight in what had been effervescing in her mind for years and now was gratified by flowers.

FOOTNOTE: I did return. In October I went once more to Courson, for the autumn Flower Show, and I stayed at the Hostellerie de St-Caprais. Beethoven had been removed, there was a bulb in the bedside lamp. But rest assured, Arlette Malgras's priorities were still in place: there was no plug for the basin.

HIS WIFE PREFERS
A QUIET LIFE

Imagine walking down a typical street of terraced houses in an ordinary town somewhere in France. The windows are closed, lace curtains hang like negative gestures precluding any insight as to what goes on in the houses. Between each front door is another faceless one, leading to the passage dividing one house from the next. Nothing holds your interest, and you might easily keep walking on, towards the outskirts of the town, until you reached the uneventful countryside of the Loiret. Except . . . except . . . there is something very anomalous about one of the doors of the undistinguished street. This door is painted; several summers have bleached the original picture to a faint outline of a sinuous tree. There is no name, no bell; not one single indication to show that you are on the threshold of brain damage. Not the sinister kind of brain damage, but a form of full frontal exposure to sights and smells which means you will never, as long as you live, clear your memory of the first time you walked through that door. Unless, of course, you are impervious to roses. In that case you will already be striding beyond the boundary of Pithiviers – which is where we are – stepping out resolutely towards Orléans with your mind on The Maid rather than on Damasks, Gallicas, Noisettes and Centifolias. If you are that sort, then I suggest you skip this chapter altogether because it is all about a fanatic, his wife and his roses.

Pithiviers, south-west of Paris, a town depending on puff pastry with a buttery almond filling for its fame, is not the sort of place you would expect a green-fingered rose-grower to be growing roses. Normandy, maybe. Or Burgundy, perhaps. Provence – obviously. But Pithiviers? The answer is, yes. Come. Push open the unmarked door, walk down the narrow passage strewn with sawdust which runs between two houses and then, if it is early to mid June, you will discover what it might be like to be a ladybird shuffling through the rose petals of a Gargantuan pot-pourri.

The day we went we were met by a cat. Unhurried, grey and white, it leant against a small tree garlanded with 'Bobbie James', a rambler of prodigious vigour which is easily confused with several other roses with pearly-white flowers and bright stamens.

This is the moment to pause. Whatever you do, do not wade in, delirious with excitement, to find yourself suffocating with roses so that you fall to the ground moaning with ecstasy at the sight of such enchantment. Take a leaf out of the cat's book and lean against a tree; hunker down; gawk; do anything to stop yourself from compulsively running forward and gobbling up roses in great greedy gulps. The pause is vital; you absolutely have to relish each moment with the finest, most highly-tuned awareness of which you are capable.

We had come to Pithiviers because the day before we had been to the Flower Show at Courson. The first display of flowers we saw as we turned left into the grounds, were his: *Les Roses Anciennes* de André Eve. Under his entry in the catalogue it said, '*André Eve aime les roses anciennes.*' If ever there was an understatement, this was it. The man is a glutton. His appetite for roses is forever unappeased, it expands in ever-widening circles of voracity. I know this because some weeks later, long after the Flower Show and after we had seen his garden for the first time, we returned to Pithiviers on the chance of finding Monsieur Eve at home so he could show us round his garden himself. Barefooted he sprang down the stairs to greet us; grabbing an umbrella he guided me out into his garden in a pouring deluge. Words, energy and impassioned fervour bowled him along as he spoke of roses with the assured conviction of a zealot, while overhead flowers and raindrops covered our hair and faces until we were weeping rose petals.

But to get back to Courson and the Flower Show. André Eve's roses were stuffed into buckets, tins and pots; gathered in bunches of profuse confusion; backed in tiers against the high walls and herded into massive galaxies of coloured chiaroscuro. In the midst of this was the man himself, standing like a bearded satyr in a grove of roses. When we could reach him, wading knee-high through his flowery progeny, he welcomed us with effusiveness and a directive. We absolutely *must* visit his rose garden the very next day. The season was exceptionally early, the roses were at their peak, and although he would not be there because he would still be at Courson, he would tell his wife to expect us. There is nothing indifferent about André Eve; his contagious gusto made us willingly acquiesce.

By the next morning, following his advice, we were at Pithiviers, walking down the street looking for number 28 faubourg d'Orléans, looking for the door with a tree painted on it. Madame Eve had been expecting us. She was as gentle and reticent as her husband was vibrant, and while we sat in a long room – half dining-, half sitting-room – with windows looking out on the garden, she told us about her husband's roses and fed Cassandra with morsels of '*Langue de Chat*'.

Rose interlaced with rose in André Eve's garden.

André Eve (who was previously a *pépinièriste*, a nurseryman, as well as a *paysagiste*, a landscape gardener) started the garden ten years ago from nothing, getting his roses from many sources: from a huge *roseraie* near Paris; from old nurseries; from private gardens; or from England. And some he has bred himself, though they are not on the market yet. He has a partner, Monsieur Jourdan, a landscape architect who is a graduate of one of France's horticultural schools, and it is he who runs the nursery which they started six years ago. A growing interest in roses has swept their business along until now there is such a demand for Old Roses that Madame Eve described her husband as having been avalanched with enquiries. To ease the situation their work is divided; Monsieur Jourdan deals with the professionals, with the bulk orders from designers and landscape architects, 'while my husband copes with private individuals.' All the business is done by post.

Travelling through Burgundy we had been surprised to discover that 'Gloire de Dijon', a rose so adored in England for its caramel petals and generous disposition, did not seem to exist for miles and miles around Dijon. Nor had any gardeners that we asked, even heard of it. André Eve was about to remedy this. He had been commissioned to supply the town of Dijon with fifteen of these most beloved roses which, in Victorian times, used to be found in every vicarage garden.

For years Old Roses have been condemned for their ephemeral flowering; all that work, all that space, merely for the brief pleasure of a transient performance. Yet no one condemns snowdrops or magnolias for their single appearance. In France, now, there really seems to be a change of attitude, a slow realization that these roses are worth eleven months of waiting.

If James Russell, that heroic rose saviour who has rescued so many old roses from extinction as well as making a superlative rose garden at Castle Howard, could see Monsieur Eve's he would be obliged to qualify his judgement that: 'You should never let a French gardener near roses – they just shave them off to ground level.' In André Eve he would find a man after his own heart.

The garden is small – only the width of the house – and about a hundred metres long. But the roses obscure the frontiers so that standing on the threshold, beside the grey and white cat, the illusion is of limitless flowers. Unlike most gardens in either France or England, here there are places enticing you to sit, with small seats half hidden under bowers, and benches placed within the embrace of shrubs. André Eve demands that you should pause for a while.

As Madame Eve explained, her husband wanted to create an intimate rose garden which at the same time would be 'wild and writhing'. In this he has succeeded. The few paths are narrow; grudgingly wide enough to allow for a little deep breathing, but where tendrils from the overhead canopy of ramblers catch at your hair as you pass. Otherwise you do writhe – in and out of roses big enough to live in. 'It is difficult to create a wild garden,' Madame Eve said, 'it's a lot of work. It is better, it is prettier – but it is a lot of work!' Yet her husband's passion for his three hundred or more different sorts of roses is intemperate. '*Il les a remis, au bout du jour, par passion, parce qu'il a trouvé ça formidable – les roses anciennes!*'

And her feelings for the garden? She admits to being *enchantée*! She finds the roses 'tremendous' – for the early morning scents, naturally, but more especially in the evening when everyone has gone and she is alone. '*On y est bien avec un bon livre.*' Madame never accompanies her husband on his travels to unearth roses, nor when he leads tours to visit gardens in Italy and England. She prefers a quiet life at home, looking after the cat and their Old English sheepdog, and listening to the hundreds of birds which inhabit the garden because neither her husband, nor their neighbours on either side, spray against aphids and blackspot.

According to William Robinson: 'The Rose is not only a "decorative" plant of the highest order, but no other plant grown in European gardens in any way approaches it in this quality.' Up to a certain point this is true. But roses badly sited can be as inappropriate as any other shrub in the garden, however intrinsically beautiful each flower may be. To fit into a garden harmoniously their form has to be taken into account. A *moyesii* appearing through the gloom of foliage throws out shock waves of radiance. But seen with its arching branches striding about a flower-bed, the vermilion petals lose their identity. Their decorative qualities are squandered.

What William Robinson does *not* tell us about these supreme plants in our gardens can lead again to disastrous siting. An attribute of roses, misunderstood until it is too late, is that each has its own particular ethos. No other genus in the garden has such a multiformity of characteristics, and unless the rose experts face us in the right direction, yearly we stumble through the summers ignorantly coping with a rose in the wrong place. Lax, lusty, pliant or bloody-minded, you have to understand their native personalities. Take 'Conrad F. Meyer', whose flowers of silvery pink emit overpowering fragrance: he is an inveterate thruster – intractable and cussed. For an easeful relationship you would be wise to know that it is not just his thorns that keep you at a distance. Or if you have succumbed to the open-cupped formation of a rose such as, say, the shell-pink Gallica 'Duchesse de Montebello', it is imperative to understand her inclination to languish. Her flowers are ravishing, her scent perfection, but unless you understand her temperament, the Duchess will be a flop.

None of this matters in André Eve's garden because the roses are gathered in such greedy armfuls – as a child gathers wild flowers and stuffs them into a jar – so that swooning roses are perforce supported by others of a more burly disposition. There is no attempt to create perspective, proportion, style or structured components. Where supports are needed for climbing roses, they are nailed together from miscellaneous pieces of wood; overflowing plants are constrained by sawn lengths of silver birch. Words like balance, relativity, layout, scale and themes do not exactly ring in your ears as you ease your way between blowsy 'Lady Hillingdon' and headstrong 'Blairi No 2'.

Against the sky, climbing up walls, straggling or threading their way up and through fruit trees or draped over pergolas, are tangles of clematis, and roses swaddling our heads with spicy, sorrelly or musky scents. 'Lord Nevill', a blue, wavy-edged clematis, twines through a white rambler, 'The Garland'. 'May Queen', another rambler, smelling of fruit salad, cavorts overhead; a velvety crimson clematis, 'Niobe', and pale lavender-coloured 'Will Goodwin' wantonly cling to the yellow roses of 'Claire Jacquier', a most compliant climber whose flowers fade to white. *Rosa gigantea*, with a scent of Tea Roses, billows in a froth of single creamy flowers, and elsewhere the large blooms of 'Vyvyan Pennell', a clematis with petals the blue of deep lavender mixed with the mauve of common lilac, sag over *treillage*.

To cover the ground, to eliminate weeding, and adding a sense of reckless prodigality which personifies André Eve's own ebulliance, are a tumult of flowers. In the midst of sedums, raspberries, hostas and yellow Jerusalem sage are roses such as a *Rosa eglanteria* with leaves smelling like a loft full of apples; a small somewhat groggy rose, 'Empereur du Maroc', with the most sumptuous-coloured flowers as deep red as a wine from Cahors. Surrounded by blue meconopsis, mulleins and Welsh poppies, forget-me-nots, asparagus and campanulas are Moss and Bourbon roses. Among the latter is demure 'Madame Pierre Oger' with chaliced flowers and petals freckled with pink. Rising above love-in-the-mist, pinks, moon daisies and clumps of rhubarb there is one of the sweetest roses, 'Céleste', with the leaden grey-green foliage of an Alba and pink scrolled buds which open into ruffled flowers delicately silvery as the light catches their outer curves. Delphiniums and geraniums curdle with foxgloves and blackish-

The reckless and boisterous planting in André Eve's back garden.

purple poppies highlighted by the white flowers of *Rosa alba semi-plena*. Colours are arbitrary; neither subtlety nor forbearance exist, but blue anchusas next to black irises next to pink roses have their own quite brilliant spontaneous combustion.

Roses bring out the worst in you. They show you up for being totally fickle and contrary. I know this to be true. I invariably become spineless when faced with single roses, whether it is the fragile petals of a *Rosa pimpinellifolia* as delicate as fine white porcelain with prickly stems and ferny foliage, or the brittle petals of *Rosa macrantha* filled with yellow stamens casting shadows as fine as etching. I know then that there can be no other roses in the world so beautiful as these single ones and my devotion is unwavering. But when I turn away towards the somnolent quartered flowers of 'Königin von Danemarck', or 'Madame Isaac Pereire' who smells like a summer pudding, my fidelity dissolves and my capitulation to these drowsy ladies is total.

Every space in this garden is filled by globular, diaphanous or flimsy petals; some are mottled, freckled or dappled, others are satiny or crinkled, velvety or matt. André Eve has created a garden out of his own unappeased ardour for roses; the suffusion of vermilion, heliotrope, azure and dead-white chaos fells your sanity in one blow. Lapped in sensuality, I defy anyone to visit this garden and not sink under a sea of adjectives.

A KITSCH GARDEN
IN THE LOT

Turning our backs on the south, where avenues of plane trees over-arch the roads for miles, and we pass from dark to light in flickering succession, where poppies spread on every scrap of desolate land like the scarlet splodges of a child using paint for the first time, we found ourselves caught up in the '*Jour de Mère*'. This is a far more serious affair than our Mothering Sunday. For one thing, the eating part of it is deadly earnest. Restaurants are booked for weeks in advance and patisseries ooze cream. The cakes, tarts and petit fours are laid out in decorative tiers on counters of glass, each one looking exquisite. Small boxes trimmed with roses and ribbons, full of sugared almonds or coloured *bon-bons*, are heaped up in little ornamental castles on the counters, and shoals of shallow tarts made with apricots and strawberries under a protective glaze, fill the windows. '*Jour de Mère*' is mother's day away from the kitchen – and nothing is too good for her.

We stopped in a small town for coffee and found the place awash with male shoppers. Frantic and profligate, as the hands on the town clock neared eleven, they bore away from flower shops eye-catching construc- tions made from flowers that only Arlette Malgras would have recognized. Young men clamped half a dozen red roses wrapped in cellophane cones onto the back of their scooters. Older men tucked carnations tied with gaudy ribbon under their arms along with the baguette. Boys sped about on bicycles delivering the final bunches of explosive roses to decorate restaurant tables.

Florist fever was at crisis point, and those sons and daughters who had lain too long in bed were left to buy any little overlooked pot of African violets they could lay their hands on. In one shop we went into we were just in time to see a daughter rather perfunctorily hand her mother four asters, accompanied by a peck on the cheek and a giggle. By eleven-twenty the florist shops were stripped and the town was deserted.

But the event was not over for us. Something unexpected and charming happened as we were having our coffee. A lady in the café, who said she lived a few doors away, presented us with a rose. She called it a giant rose.

It was. It had the largest, most lax, bilious-yellow petals, edged with a frill of maroon, that I had ever seen. 'My garden is nothing. But this rose is a *monstre!*' We agreed. 'I shall have to cut it down in the autumn.'

In our quest for gardens there had been no standard set as to which to include and which to exclude. Often when we stopped somewhere for the night I would ask the proprietor of the hotel about gardens in the locality. Usually it led to places without much merit. Yet you can never tell. As I did not want to narrow my choice to just those kind of gardens which are universally admired, or which conform to English taste, I knew I had to be receptive and throw out feelers here and there, to take on gardeners burning with passion – whatever their taste – as well as those with flawless discretion. If the gardeners had flair but their gardens were not the way I would have made them, *tant pis*. They were French.

So when one day I was buying one of those marvellous dark green watering cans which we often bring back from France, and I asked the shopkeeper about local gardens, it was an auspicious moment. Standing beside me was a stout, jolly lady who burst into our conversation by telling me she had a '*tellement ravissant*' garden and would I like to visit it as it was nearby and she would be delighted. How could I refuse? We arranged that we would call that afternoon.

On arrival we rescued a hedgehog. The drama of this event made us instantly chummy. The poor animal, not yet fully grown, was paddling pathetically round and round a small ornamental pool just inside the decorative gates. None of us could reach into the centre to retrieve it, nor could we pick it up with a couple of long canes used like a pair of giant chopsticks. A bucket? Madame hurried to the house while we supported the hedgehog from drowning on a bamboo. It was touch and go for a few minutes; when we did eventually put the bedraggled creature on the grass, madame told us it was the first time she had seen *un hérisson* in the garden in twenty-six years.

Twenty-six years ago she and her husband had built the house on the outskirts of a small town in the Grand Périgord Quercy. The town was not distinguished by anything architecturally special; like so many handsome French towns it was built on a hill. From the encircling road radiating lanes led up to the church on the top. Here twice a week was a market selling local honey, garlic and 'black' wine. On the circular road, once a week, was a market selling hideous mass-produced clothes, delightful old-fashioned kitchen aprons made of flowery cotton, and more bedroom slippers than seemed reasonable. Just below this road, where the hill slanted down to a stream and a modest chapel picturesquely sited beside a weir, was madame's house.

Either side of the entrance, on concrete pillars, were two large pots with a conifer in each. 'When we bought the land there was nothing. You see here, there is a little *bassin* – I don't know what you call it – but not until some time later did my husband and I discover it.' The pool had been totally obscured by long grass and, as Madame put it, the land was very ugly. 'My son likes gardening,' she said with pride; it was he who had planted an Irish yew, a weeping birch, irises and nasturtiums around the pool. And when he can he leaves his work as an economic analyst in Paris, and visits his mother and grandmother, bringing some 'extraordinary or exotic plant with him'.

As we walked with Madame we were joined by her mother. She was deaf, but though she was unable to hear what her daughter was saying, she smiled with obvious pleasure at the occasion. 'My old mother, who is eighty-six, spends two hours each morning on her toilette. I'm not joking. She must appear *soignée*! Her hair, her skin, her dress. At her age!' Madame thought it hilarious. 'She loves her toilette – but me, I love my garden. Look!' We could hardly do otherwise, for in front of us, standing among ageratums, zinnias, lilies and marigolds was a pre-cast statue of Proserpine, flanked by 'classical' columns made of concrete. One was broken, its top half tumbled artistically onto the lawn. '*Alors ça*,' and she pointed to some more concrete blocks, 'those are to go on the top. My son is doing it. *Petit à petit* on each visit. He has a lot of taste, he does really. And those,' indicating a double row of six cement bases, where her son's enthusiasm had overcome discrimination, 'those are going to make a *boulevard* of columns!' The whole production was of such indelicate and kitsch ingenuity it was impossible not to enter into the spirit of the place, and her excitement was so contagious it was easy to join in with her: '*oh, là, là! Quel spectacle!*'

The garden was a rectangle about a hundred and fifty feet long by sixty feet wide, with a concrete path, wide enough to take a car, running straight to the house. Either side were large vases the grey colour of brains, filled with sweet williams and petunias. In the centre of the lawn a magnolia was about to flower. 'Normally it flowers in July, but this year things are early.' Then she added with obvious glee, 'I'm going to put electricity into the magnolia to make *un spectacle*.' She pointed to the asters, which should not be flowering until September but which she thinks will be out in July. 'But my spiraea – this year – it hasn't had a single flower. Normally it's like a mound of snow.' Yet her 'Boule de Neige' was a fantastic sight of white globular petals, covering the shrub with abundant recklessness. '*Une splendeur*! It's never been so beautiful.' But the cistus had failed her, so had another magnolia. 'I haven't had one single flower.' The winter and spring had been exceptionally dry. 'We've had no water at all. The flowers have suffered terribly.' She showed us some forlorn coreopsis and some other late summer plants. Unless the dahlias could pull it round I could see the season, in her eyes, might be a wash-out. 'I have two hundred dahlias. So when they're in flower everyone stops to look because they're so beautiful. There are so many, so many.' She waved her arms about in all directions, '*Il y'en a! Il y'en a! Il y'en a!*' I could imagine. If ever a garden was suited to dahlias, this one was. They could roar their heads off in outrageous colours and look wonderful while onlookers would be driven back gasping for air. What a shame to miss it.

'I work *toute la journée* in the garden. I have a very large house but I work all the time outside. My husband has been dead a year, so I must . . . I'm naughty. I never spend time doing housework!' Her husband had liked painting and only worked in the garden when help was needed, and even then 'not with enthusiasm. *Voilà*.' Beside us was a swathe of mauve and plum-coloured poppies, the double, fluffy ones, in front of a sweet-scented rose with small, bright pink flowers. 'My son knows its name – but I don't.' She pointed to another rose still in bud, '*Oh, elle est belle! Violette et double. Elle est belle, belle, belle*! Here I have a white one, but she's not so pretty.' She led us to a flower bed running along the front of the house where there were hollyhocks and verbascums planted around a flamboyant crimson rose with a brilliant yellow vortex. 'I call that the cocktail rose. She's old – twenty-six years I've had her.' She described her plans for making a pergola along the side of the house, for planting wisterias and for finding more roses. 'This year for the first time I shall plant old roses, very old roses.'

We followed her to the back of the house to see her vegetable garden. 'I make it out of habit – because my mother and I don't really need all this . . .' She indicated the small rows of tomatoes, lettuces, courgettes and spinach. There was a pungent smell from thyme and sages growing beside mint, parsley and celery. She gestured towards the lovage: 'It's only good with tomatoes, otherwise it's too strong.' Among the shallots and chives, their beds edged with mignonettes, were carnations to pick for the house. 'They smell so lovely in the evening. And this is a thornless blackberry. You see she doesn't prick, and she's laden with fruit for at least two or three months. We love it. When my daughter comes to stay we make a dessert. It's very presentable.'

Her pleasure in the garden was infectious and ingenuous; she was the sort of gardener who had the confidence to believe in what she was doing, and no amount of sophisticated advice was going to deflect her from making her garden just the way she wanted it. As we walked back towards the gate along the other side of the garden we passed beds of delphiniums interplanted with dark red roses; a syringa about to flower surrounded by bright yellow, double nasturtiums; Jacob's ladder, marigolds and 'a white rose that's not *vilain*,' not bad-looking. '*Là*, there are pretty plants – oxalis – but they're not in flower yet.' Like all truly seasoned gardeners, she passed her own epithet on her garden. Her last words to us as we left were, 'Come back – a little later on. Now there is nothing . . . I have nothing!'

Their Latin Names
Painted in White

Poitou, Bordelais, Guyenne and Gascogne have such a rhythmic lilt that I was almost reconciled to turning my back on the great heartland of France. But it was an effort. And such a long way, too. As the land became flatter the further west we drove, where the verges were interlaced with bright pink vetch, my spirit drooped and I wondered if we were right to follow up such a tenuous introduction. We had been given the briefest hint. A name, an island . . . but what we would find there would be unique – like nowhere else to be found in France. It was tempting, of course, but by doing this huge trek were we perhaps missing a hundred garden gems within touching distance of each other in the lushness of the Loire? France has this effect. Its diversity of terrain makes me covetous to know it all, even the suppurating alleys of southern cities or the industrial towns in Flanders festering in their own pollution.

The brothers we were to visit had no telephone; and the local Syndicat d'Initiative was not informative. They did not really have the answers to our questions about distances and transport on the island, where cars were prohibited, but were vaguely hopeful that we would find a horse and carriage at the quayside. They gave us the ferry timetable.

It was overcast and muggy as we left the harbour at 8.15 next morning. This was the first ferry of the day and it was obvious that almost every traveller was an habitué. A man in a dark suit carrying a briefcase stood out like a sore thumb; the rest, in spite of greeting each other familiarly, were a taciturn lot. Boxes of sardines, begonias, bread, tomatoes, a surprising number of dogs and a couple of motor-bikes were crammed onto the small open deck where we sat on wet benches trying to shelter Cassandra from a blustery wind. Ozone went to our heads, while the age old smell of fish, tar and seaweed, wet wood and brine laced with Gauloise, and the grating scream of scavaging gulls, seemed far from the scented tranquillity of Provence.

Lofty pine trees dominated the quay of the little island, which had fewer than two hundred inhabitants. And immense hollyhocks, pink, yellow and cream, growing wild down the main street of the village, stood as tall as the

The brothers live below ground level surrounded by specimen exotica.

cottages, diminutive and charming, which were painted in pale washes of blue, green and primrose.

The brothers lived at the other end of the island, only about two or three kilometres away, we were told – which, had we been travelling without a baby, would have been no problem. But when the horse and carriage turned out to be a rubber-tyred tumbril with benches for about twenty passengers drawn by two shire horses, and the road petered out long before our destination, we looked for bicycles. We found them for hire at the general store, but a harness to attach Cassandra onto the back was asking too much. We were sent here and there looking for some kind of strap that would do. It was useless; in the end we used a long cotton sash I was wearing to bind her like a limp, indeterminate soft toy to the bicycle. Tamsin led the way; I followed, keeping my eyes steadfastly on Cassandra's wobbling back to warn Tamsin every time her daughter slumped in sleep.

We had been waved vaguely down the coast, so when the road gave up we cycled along paths which drew us further and further into wilderness. Forced by sand and tree roots to push the bicycles through a deepening tangle of undergrowth, we became imprisoned by the wild coast, deserted and rocky on one side, shrubs and sighing pines on the other. If only then, at the nadir of our desperation, we had known we were about to find one of the most outlandish, distinguished and eccentric 'gardens' of our journey, our resolve might not have faltered.

A two-foot high sign saying PRIVÉ behind an unscalable wire fence lifted our spirits no end. This must be it. And not until we actually faced the gate, tightly bound against intruders, did we lose our nerve. Then, overcome by doubt and apprehension at our audacity, insensitivity and misplaced boldness, we did hesitate. It was a bad moment. Miles away, at the Flower Show at Courson, Paul's name written into our notebook had held no reality, but now, standing outside the fence, we faced it; and the fact that no house was visible, that there might be dogs intended for people like us, and that we had arrived unannounced, all added to our sense of intimidation. But the struggle we had gone through, wasting a precious hour, gave us the courage to unwire the gate, push our bicycles through into the unkempt scrub, lay them under a bush and walk on.

Oh, the unexpected solace of being welcomed. I suppose we did not look very threatening, but not for a second did Jean hesitate or seem at all thrown at the sight of the three of us. In fact his courtesy and warmth were so spontaneous, we even felt he was glad to see us. Sitting us down on a plank of wood in the shade, he went to find his brother Paul who was working somewhere on the land. In a few moments he appeared, smiling, with tousled white hair, wiping his hands on his sleeve after rinsing them in a bucket before offering us his elbow to shake. We felt we had arrived in paradise! Such felicity, such impromptu cordiality, and our own relief at having found them and their extraordinary garden, made us grin like idiots.

For some reason Tamsin and I had both expected to find that Paul was an eccentric aristocrat, who had become a botanical recluse. What we found were two brothers both in their mid-to-late seventies, one of whom had been a *patissier* from the Châteauroux region and the other a dentist. 'He was initiated to gardening years ago, madame – he used to pull teeth,' Paul explained, 'but now, *eh bien*, he pulls weeds.'

Thirty years ago Paul, who had hankered all his life after making a garden of challenging plants, had bought two and a half hectares at the far end of the island. Here, protection from other islands and the lowness of the terrain meant he could build up a collection of rare and exotic plants in a relatively temperate climate. 'I started here slowly, well a little, and then in 1965 I stayed here.' Their land, which once had belonged to the military, had never been cultivated but remained a formless waste of gorse, the white *Cistus salvifolius* with leaves looking like sage, a fragrant evergreen, *Phillyrea angustifolia*, which looks a bit like holm oak, and brambles. In the past, the rest of the island must have been highly productive to support a garrison of at least four hundred men.

Undeterred by the chaos he faced, Paul's original and effective method of coping with the derelict land was simple – he razed to the ground every single unwanted shred of undergrowth. After that he planted everywhere a copious mixture of cistus grown from seeds brought back from Cannes and Nice, which he then covered with the tangled bramble and gorse debris to protect the young seedlings from the cold and heat. As Paul so elegantly put it, 'The earth did us the honour of becoming enriched from the contribution of vegetable and animal manure.' In the end the effect was magical; the land blossomed with magenta and rose, pink and crimson, white with blotches of purple, from the papery petals of thousands of cistus. Then he began to plant. Olives, cypress, eucalyptus and an Atlas cedar, a loquat from Japan, pines from Spain and Greece; the absurdly realistic 'bottle brush' trees – callistemons from Australia, whose scarlet, yellow or creamy flowers grow on cylindrical spikes; and catalpas with their frilly-edged flowers, large bright leaves and seed pods dangling like narrow runner-beans.

He planted twining actinidias; a silk vine, *Periploca graeca*, with greenish flowers on the outside and purply-brown within; a tender dogwood, *Cornus capitata*, a small tree of outstanding distinction from the Himalayas with flowerheads surrounded by sulphur-yellow bracts; a *Eucryphia* x *hillieri* ('it suffered by being kept by the customs too long'). Eucryphias are trees of such exquisite beauty that I would give anything to be able to grow one. Tall, sometimes reaching twenty feet in height, but no more than about six or seven feet wide, their whole length in summer is covered with an extravagant froth of white flowers, so profuse and lush with their bright yellow stamens that involuntarily you gasp in disbelief.

Others Paul cherishes for their fortitude are an *Arbutus arizonica* with foxy-red peeling bark; *Crinodendron patagua*, a South American tree with white, bell-shaped flowers; an *Escallonia viscosa*, a resinous shrub with clusters of pendulous white flowers, and a strange leathery-leafed tree with sweet, edible fruit, *Peumus boldus*. His *Melianthus major*, an evergreen shrub with tawny, tubular flowers, which rarely blooms in Britain because of its delicate nature, is described by Christopher Lloyd, in *The Well-Tempered Garden*, as a ravishing plant well worth the effort of lifting in autumn and overwintering indoors.

Pinus coulteri, Rhododendron occidentale and a Chinese pistachio are equally admired for their survival, along with two South American colletias, *C. armata* and *C. cruciata*. 'So, you see,' Paul rather ruefully remarked, 'I am forced to learn the capabilities of the plants which will grow here!'

The fort, where the brothers live, is a low building crouching like a great grey, prehistoric creature festooned with climbers and surrounded by a hotch-potch collection of pots full of seedlings. 'This *batterie*,' Paul explained a bit apologetically, 'was where there were cannon to prevent the British navy entering the bay, and there were ten cannon which were under the little wall you see.'

Paul and Jean never leave the island. A weekly visit to the village where we landed provides them with all they need. They seldom have visitors but they do fear for the island. 'The tourists pick everything,' Paul lamented, '*les chardons bleu, les oeillets* (blue thistles and pinks) – everything. They'll have to be reintroduced. Perhaps we'll do it.'

Below ground level, we sat talking in their kitchen while they looked after us with charming concern to find drinks and comfort. Books on gardening, plant catalogues and botanical dictionaries, cuttings from newspapers, nails, sellotape and candles, *un bonnet de laine* and gardening tools cluttered up the long table and various sagging shelves. At one end was a sink and behind a curtain was where they slept. In the middle of the room stood what looked like a very primitive contraption, with a long pipe

Donkeys keep down the garrigue when it threatens to overwhelm the trees.

sticking out of it and a mantle on the top. It was a large gas cylinder; they have no electricity. 'We have a windmill, it works well in winter – but there is little wind at present.' Then, laughing with casual acceptance of the way things are, Paul added, 'so it's lucky the days are long. Yes, it's lucky the days are long.'

Later, walking through the unkempt grass where their donkeys are used as lawn-mowers to keep down the paths, and sea shells are scattered when the ground becomes muddy, Paul pushed ahead, pulling aside undergrowth to show us some wonderful, vulnerable, rare, temperamental or way-out plant that he had grown from seed. The donkeys, he explained to us, he dare not put out much except in winter because, not surprisingly, they eat plants they should not. 'But at present I put them on a piece of abandoned land, a place a little bit different – not a wood, not undergrowth exactly, but rather like Mediterranean *garrigue*. And I don't understand why there should be this Mediterranean part – the *garrigue* just here.'

Garrigue is not the same as *maquis*, or scrub, which grows on acid soil. The *garrigue* appears on limestone. It spreads along the foot of the more ancient parts of the Massif Central. Where the rock has not been entirely laid waste by erosion resulting from man's destruction, holm oaks and Aleppo pines, cistus, gorse, scrub oak and asphodels survive amongst the wilderness of aromatic plants.

Paul and Jean water nothing apart from *les élevages*, but after that, 'Once I've planted them outside I water no more. *Eh bah*, if they die they aren't in the right place. If they're happy, they're happy and one can go on.' What an enviable philosophy. What strength of mind and courage to accept the inevitable with his plants and not crave endlessly to try and re-try to grow against the grain of the climate.

His enthusiasm was irrepressible; in spite of wearing a rough tweed jacket and wellingtons on such a mild day, he leapt vigorously ahead like an excited child, picking at every aromatic plant to please us with its fragrance. For a botanist it would be heaven and I felt hopelessly inadequate in not having the knowledge to appreciate just how remarkable some of his plants must be. Hens and their tiny chicks appeared all over the place from out of the *garrigue*. As Paul and Jean seldom search for the eggs and they do not have a vegetable garden, I could understand why he said rather wearily, 'We eat chicken and chicken and chicken . . .'

Rusty iron doors served as bridges across narrow ditches, planks used as seats were propped up on stones; a home-made ladder with tapering ends was held together by thongs of tubing; nothing had been dug over, trimmed or manicured; nothing was for show, for subtleties of colour or design, for the harmony of careful positioning. It was a place for rarity and thriving; for the sake of the plants themselves and nothing else. Every single thing, even those hidden deep within the scrub and tattered grasses, had been carefully labelled, with their Latin names painted in white on strips cut from old car tyres.

Arbutus, genista, escallonias and spiraea; species roses, the lovely Winter's bark, *Drimys winteri*, milk-white and fragrant; japonica, buddleias and myrtle, lavender, madonna lilies, ferns and pistachio are among some of Paul's plants, as well as the clianthus with their scarlet claws, and the sea daffodil, *Pancratium maritimum*, whose natural habitat is around the Mediterranean. Theophrastus, the fourth century BC author of the *History of Plants*, recorded the beguiling fact that the woolly hairs found on the inside of the seed-coat of sea daffodils, were used to weave felt shoes. Felt shoes! For heaven's sake, how many seed pods would be needed for just one toe, and how on earth did one gather the 'woolly hairs' anyway?

Wherever we walked, crowded into groups or pushed into the shade were rusty buckets, discarded saucepans, tins cut in half, jars and plastic pots, anything that would hold a handful of earth and a seedling. In wooden crates Jean showed us minute cuttings, each one protected by an upturned glass jar covered with black netting. And somewhere incongruously, from out of an old tyre grew a slender, clear, lilac-rose *Geranium napuligerum*, its frailty emphasised by its container.

Paul is still looking for seeds, including those of *Arbutus andrachne*, of *Eucalyptus vernicosa* and *Tagetes lucida*; we were unable to find them for him in England though Chiltern Seeds in Cumbria were able to supply *Xanthonhoea australis*, the Australian Grass-Tree, and *Yucca whipplei* with gigantic panicles of greenish-white flowers. By now I hope they are well-rooted and headed for summer.

The brothers pressed us to stay for lunch, in fact Jean was already walking about peeling a potato in preparation for a meal. But we had squandered that precious hour in losing our way. We had to leave. We had to catch the early afternoon ferry to keep next day's gardening engagement which was far away. Like Robert Frost we had promises to keep, and miles to go before we slept.

At home in a drawer I have a bag in which I still have some of the aromatic pieces which Paul picked for us. Whenever I smell their crumbling legacy – a laurel from Chile or a bay from California – they remind me instantly of the wide sky, the ocean and the presence of those two men who live a life far beyond the boundaries of our usual complexities.

JARDINS
RAFFINÉS

'THEY OPEN THEIR EYES WIDE'

Normandy is not an area of France I know well. Memories of returning northwards in late October past small orchards still full of apples on apple trees, surrounding half-timbered cottages, were all I had to go on. I knew that parts of it were haunted by Proust and Flaubert with their evocative descriptions of the countryside, but where we were going was to Basse Normandie, to an area called Pays de Bocage. Bocage here means farmland criss-crossed with hedges and trees, scattered with villages. The scene was peaceful, with cows lying under fruit trees placidly chewing the cud and poplar trees adding soft verticals to the landscape. A row of them, severely pollarded, lined the path up to a cottage door, their leaves still that delicate green and bronze of young growth.

We stayed the night at Villers-Bocage and next morning our route took us through a village where the width of the main street was on such a majestic scale we thought we must be trespassing. This was Balleroy. And the impressive drive from the steps of the Château de Balleroy, a seventeenth-century bit of classical splendour, runs straight as a die through parkland, through the gates and right through the village to the far side. No wonder we felt disorientated.

The garden we had come to see was one belonging to a nursery – Planbessin. Surely a garden with a nursery is the most persuasive form of salesmanship for anyone who has a piece of earth and the innocence to enter such a place? Few gardeners can resist. It is only the visitors without a garden, those who take a vicarious delight in what other people do with flowers, who can leave such places empty-handed. Near where I live in Shropshire there is one such garden and nursery, Stone House Cottage Garden, where the walls are covered with radiant climbers and the hedged compartments are so packed with floral inducements, that even before I cross the threshold reason has fled and I succumb.

But in France? I wondered. Although in Courson we had been told that Planbessin was one of the most prestigious nursery gardens in France, judging by the *pépinières* we had seen in other parts of the country, I felt sceptical. Would it be mostly conifers? Those appalling cultivars, either frosted, glaucous, viridian or the greenish-yellow of addled eggs; those deformed and tortured growths that sidle over the ground as proof that the gardener has run out of ideas? Would there be rows of user-friendly flowers with most space given over to that holy cow of French gardening – the dahlia?

What an over-opinionated and narrow-minded critic I was with my preconceptions. Planbessin was not remotely like this, and I felt guiltily apologetic towards the extremely erudite Frenchman who had suggested we visit it.

For a first encounter with a garden – surely this one at Planbessin must be the most original in the world? We might have been forgiven for imagining we had taken a wrong turn and landed up in a piggery. Apart from barking dogs which hurled themselves at us as we opened the car doors, the effluent smell of ammonia and piercing stench of pig manure hit us in the face like tangible smog. The place is a working pig-farm. Only in the last fifteen years have Colette and Hubert Sainte-Beuve started their nursery. Pigs and flowers! What a brilliant combination. Their juxtaposition has dynamic impact. And as my husband and I used once to keep one or two pigs, animals for which I have a low smouldering devotion, I thought with these extremes of smells I was in heaven.

At the entrance, as we walked over lovely slabs of slate and contrasting brick, was *une tonnelle* – a wooden bower all pretty and romantic – covered with clematis, ceanothus and honeysuckles and with enough delicious fragrance to allow us immediately to change olfactory mood. The garden, which had been made out of one hectare of apple orchard surrounded by high hornbeam hedges, was only three years old. The Sainte-Beuves had been provoked into making it as an addition to their nursery, '. . . to show the French how to make a garden. We want it to be beautiful,' said Colette Sainte-Beuve, 'but at the same time *educatif*, so that people can see, if they have a pond, for instance, which plants would be suitable.'

Within the pages of their extensive catalogue, Monsieur and Madame Sainte-Beuve describe their attitude to their new garden as '*le fruit d'une passion, celle du jardin et de l'amour des plantes.*' The introduction goes on to say how a garden must be intimate; a place suitable for contemplation; a place to be shared. Above all it must be a reflection of the gardener's own personality. The standard is set.

Colette Sainte-Beuve told us that before her husband drew the first designs for the two pools – the rectangular and the hexagonal ones – the garden had been *en tête*. The pools are the focal points around which everything slowly took shape. The layout is arranged so that the perennials in the nursery can be seen performing in carefully designed settings in the garden. Each enclosure displays the plant to its best.

Divided by shrubs, hedges and trees – including viburnums, maples, magnolias and cherries – each garden shows off plants suitable for a different setting: aquatic, scented, heather, culinary, plants for mixed borders and so on. Two compartments, still in an unsettled state, are an '*amphithéâtre, vous voyez?*' made of railway sleepers, with a fine collection of hydrangeas, which does not yet please her, and a Japanese garden with a decorative pagoda and suitably exotic plants. 'We'll change the Japanese garden . . . the plants are not yet right.'

And why is there so little stone used in French gardens? 'You don't see much stone used in France,' said Madame Sainte-Beuve, 'except perhaps in the "*jardins à la française*" – formal, and without flowers.'

But stone is essential to a garden. Those gardens made without a framework, a skeleton of stone, wood or brick leave you with a hungry sense of dissatisfaction; with an awareness that something is missing. It may not be until long afterwards that you remember why a particular garden had no flavour. Flowers were there in abundance, but flowers, shrubs and trees are not enough to make a garden. You need only look at a Jekyll/Lutyens production, even if only in a book, to see that what makes it leap from the page is the unity between plants and static weight.

The plentiful use of stone at Planbessin was local slate, and limestone slabs that came from further afield. Paving surrounded the long rectangular pool, with waterlilies floating on its dark, reflective surface. Plants tumbled over the edges, growing in and out of water. 'On one side it's a little bit planted according to colour, with purplish plants and there yellow, there white – *enfin*, there's a bit of mixing.' On the other side were primulas, including 'Inverewe' which detonated the shade with brilliance, and *Hosta sieboldiana* 'Frances Williams', which has lime-yellow edging to its sculptured leaves. The majority of gardeners were wringing their hands over the lack of water after two dry winters and a dry spring, but at Planbessin it is never a problem. From the nearby river a constant source of water can be pumped for irrigation; for topping-up the pools; for the large pots and for supplying an *évier de pierre*, a stone sink.

The mixed borders, with a wide grass path running straight down the centre towards a bench and a view of undramatic countryside, are full of tall herbaceous plants at the back of the bed, coming forward to low-growing mounds. It was very pretty, and very English. On the shaded side of the garden Madame Sainte-Beuve grows day-lilies and irises ('I don't like irises very much; they're over so quickly and their leaves aren't

One of the pools used to show varieties of waterside planting.

interesting') and plants with decorative leaves to capture maximum sunlight, like astrantias, peonies, acanthus and stephanandras.

Horizontal tedium is relieved by the vertical impact of trees. Trees such as conifers, a twisted willow, a *Pyrus salicifolia* or a catalpa with flowers like foxgloves add another dimension, providing contrasting silhouettes, solid mass and graphic control. There are small groups of alders, birches, elders, sorbus and willows.

Nowhere in France had we seen any 'architectural' grass cutting, where designs are made from cutting the grass to different lengths, or where patches of wild flowers are allowed to seed with mown paths running between them. 'No, it's true,' said Madame Sainte-Beuve, 'there isn't much wildness in gardens. I've noticed in England particularly, how rough grass is left with wild flowers growing in it.' And species bulbs? No, she did not grow many bulbs – a few fritillaries, jonquils, tulips, 'One variety of tulip – a double pink one. And also I have narcissus and cyclamen. *Voilà!*'

The herb garden is surrounded by yew. The hedge seemed remarkably mature for a young garden, until Colette Sainte-Beuve explained that the yews had been planted before they started – as a confident gesture into the future because they knew one day they would make a garden of '*les plantes condimentaires et officinales*'. Among the medicinal and culinary plants which we had universally found in French herb gardens were some less common: wild ginger, hart's tongue, evening primrose, 'cat's foot', comfrey and great burnet.

Primarily the garden is for hardy plants, both common and uncommon. Plants much loved by Colette Sainte-Beuve are *Sanguisorba canadensis,* with spikes of white flowers protruding from pale pinnate leaves, chocolate-scented *Cosmos atrosanguineus,* whose petals are the deep red of garnets, and one of that magnificent family of lilies, *Crinum* x *powellii,* out of whose strap-like leaves appear pale pink flowers with a brush-stroke of damask down each petal. Among the shrubs is a favourite clematis, *C. heracleifolia davidiana,* very beautiful, with flowers the colour of bleached bluebells.

As the number of different plants displayed in the garden at Planbessin is over fifteen hundred, I will name some of those grown for specific environments to give an idea of what this nursery can offer. In rockeries and low walls Madame Sainte-Beuve suggests carline thistles, willow herb, balloon flowers and ballota – a woolly plant whose seed vessels are still used as floating wicks for oil lamps in wayside shrines in Greece.

To cover the ground there are cinquefoil, bergenia, lungwort, gypsophila and the indispensable nepetas; for damp and cool places are the wand flower, foxgloves, monkshood, maidenhair and royal ferns; in the shade or in north-facing beds the nursery includes columbines, pearl everlasting, goat's rue, peony and turtle-head.

On chalky soil where the plants often have a silvery reflection and a bluish leafage like carnations, Colette Sainte-Beuve supplies plume poppies, speedwell, meadow-rue, lavender, delphiniums and asphodels – not the kind that grow on overgrazed land around the Mediterranean forming a film like a smoky-pink cataract, but the asphodels with fragrant yellow spears and grassy leaves.

And for gardeners whose soil is sticky, she says, '*Si, en hiver, la terre colle à vos pieds* but in summer turns to rock, try bergamot, michaelmas daisy, self-heal, lady's mantle, and the regal compass plant from the prairies of America whose leaves, when young, orientate themselves north and south. But for sandy soil, where compost is essential and autumn planting is wise, she advises planting mullein, Jacob's ladder, arabis and cistus.

Poetically, she says of coastal gardens where plants must withstand wind and salt, '*Elles sont avides de la lumière qui tombe du ciel et qui reflète dans l'eau.*' Plants such as these, eager for sunlight and reflections off the sea, are honeysuckle, mallow, tree lupin, fuchsia and red hot pokers. Then she has her '*passe-partout*' plants, those buddleias, anemones, crocosmias and potentillas which tolerate either chalk, sand, clay or acid soil; drought or damp, sun or shade.

Innumerable plants are there for scent; for aquatic or boggy places, which include a wonderful collection of ferns; for those whose taste is for drying flowers; or for long-lasting plants with decorative foliage which '*ornent le jardin presque toute l'année*'.

As for her '*grandes plantes*', such as yellow ox-eye, ornamental rhubarb, gunnera and some of the euphorbias, Madame Sainte-Beuve recommends that with their dimension and their architectural form they merit a well-chosen place to emphasize the culminating point of a bed; or they should be seen in isolation; or as a background screen at the garden's boundaries.

No wonder French gardeners visiting Planbessin are bowled over. As Colette Sainte-Beuve said, 'The geranium! When they see that it's a perennial flower they open their eyes wide. For them the geranium is a pelargonium – the one to put in front windows!' They stare amazed to see a *Geranium eriostemon* with muddy violet flowers, or a magenta patch of ground covered with G. x *riversleaianum* 'Russell Prichard', or the prettiest thing with clear blue flowers with white centres, G. *wallichianum* 'Buxton's Blue'. 'It's always the same things planted in French gardens. Not much imagination!' In order to stop them in their tracks, she has a small explosive pink rose, 'Yolande d'Aragon', with a thrusting carriage, positioned deliberately to contrast with the cavernous dark green of an ilex.

In the garden's lush atmosphere and inexhaustible display, every visitor is captive; they inevitably buy more than they intended. 'The French spend money on their houses, but not on their gardens. Gardens come second – so people do the minimum. They don't yet seek to improve their gardens . . . soon, they will!' Colette Sainte-Beuve's educational zealotry is working slowly. Cautiously she adds, 'Bit by bit it's changing. The French are not used to seeing gardens like this – but they like it. The first thing they say is: "Ah, it must be a lot of work!" But it's not.' Because the plants are so densely planted there is little weeding to do. What is necessary and absolutely crucial to the well-being of the whole garden is mulching. Pigs! I wondered. Would all that pungent pig manure slowly rot until one day it reappeared as a scented rose or a medley of penstemons?

Colette Sainte-Beuve goes to England to visit gardens as often as she can. In particular she loves Sissinghurst Castle and Beth Chatto's garden. Every year she goes to the two shows at Courson. 'I've been going since the beginning – eight years, I think.' Has it changed? 'Yes, I think it has. Years ago, when there were fewer people, it was less commercial, whereas now people buy-in plants to sell.' And Chelsea? 'It's artificial. Personally I don't like Chelsea.' Hurray, hurray. It was a treat to hear an erudite and knowledgeable gardener pass judgement on such a hallowed institution. Speaking from her heart as well as her head, and endearing her to me forever, she put succinctly the final reason for her dismissal of the Chelsea Flower Show: 'I used to like Chelsea in earlier times because the Englishwomen wore such extraordinary hats. It was very amusing – I loved it. But now Englishwomen no longer wear hats – so I no longer go.'

Visitors are intended to linger in the garden at Planbessin.

'I WAS PLEASED WHEN YOU SAID "AH"'

Odile Masquelier, having read my book about making a garden in the hills of southern Shropshire, wrote saying: 'My garden is completely different. Warm, burning in summer. On a hill – certainly more protected in winter – dominating the city of Lyon, about two acres of old-fashioned roses, clematis and perennials. Thick lime and stones – the bed of the old Rhône river. But no stream, no running water, all that I have always dreamed about.'

She need have no regrets. What she has made in the city lacks nothing. Running water, twining through a fold of land in England, means frost – that startling and ravishing killer that turns the familiar into a brittle, finely wrought etching. Here, instead, where the city of Lyon could be distantly seen through trees and where the traffic sounded like the continual low undertow of the sea, frost fell away and Odile had no need to plead with her plants not to come into bud too soon after a warm winter.

Lyon, important for its manufacture of silk since the sixteenth century, has the fascination of having two great rivers converging on it: the majestic and powerful Rhône, which turns towards the south at Lyon, and the Saône, whose placid meander originates in the green serenity of the Vosges. *La Mulatière* district of the city, where Georges and Odile Masquelier have their garden, is on the south-western slopes where tiny lanes twist their way between high walls and where the handsome houses are secluded and verdurous. It is easy to imagine how countrified this part of Lyon must have been until recently. The *chemin Fontanières*, which is where the Masquelier family live, was an old Roman way, and Odile tells us she still occasionally unearths Roman fragments as she digs.

The first view of the garden as we entered the house, was one of distant sunlight and flowers. The effect was tantalizing. Like pins to a magnet we were drawn willy-nilly towards the garden. At that time of year it was pink and white tulips that lured us onto the terrace. Under the house, with its thick pelt of Virginia creeper, were pale pink peonies against a background of speckled trees coming into leaf and the murky stillness of huge conifers. To the right, running parallel with the garden wall, was a wide flower-bed and a long pergola where roses, not yet in flower, would soon draw other visitors towards the garden. Odile is far too fastidious a gardener to have achieved this first view of the garden by chance. Every prospect and vista, every small group of plantings, was carefully handled and subtly worked out. 'I knew I must have a mixed border here,' said Odile, 'to see immediately you enter the house. So I was pleased when you said "Ah" – because that's what I wanted!'

Monsieur and Madame Masquelier started their garden twenty-five years ago in a modest way. Three catalpa trees, some pines, a cedar and an orchard were what they had to go on, as well as an *allée* of sycamores. These had to be banished. Gardens and sycamores lack symbiosis; the greedy roots of the trees reach everywhere; their shade is dense, and they have a habit of dispersing seedlings as liberally as a dandelion spreads its fluff.

'When we first came we couldn't see the city, but later when someone bought the house below us they cut down all the trees. One morning we just woke up – and we were desperate. It seemed as though we were right on the station.' This was the *Gare Perrache*, the main station in the heart of the city. But that was not all. A few days before we came to visit her, a gale had felled an ancient and magnificent willow tree. Odile was heart-broken. It had left a huge hole, revealing the city where before there had been shelter and the sibilant sound of leaves. Even so her jubilant spirit would not let her grieve for long. 'Come here, this is nice!' And she pointed. 'That is the *Dôme de la Part-Dieu* and it looks to me like Florence. On Sunday morning you can hear the sound of church bells!'

The same positive vigour is summed up by her philosophy towards the garden: 'Everything follows a very simple principle. I grow what grows here . . . and what seeds itself.' Chance seedlings that please her are allowed to stay, others are moved, maybe several times, until finally the right place is found for them. Her major enemy is drought. 'The garden's on clay, slightly alkaline,' Odile explained, 'and when you make a hole you dig out stones and clay. So I put in tons of *tourbe* – how do you say? Peat? Every time I plant I put in some peat. In springtime, in fall, all the time.' Tiresome setbacks, not perhaps so dire as drought or wind, are the mice which eat the tulips and squirrels which dig up her cyclamen. And ivy, infiltrating everywhere, is an annual scourge.

When she first began the garden Odile made flower arrangements as a way of earning money, but in the end it became too exhausting. 'To grow, to pick – and it takes a long, long time to prepare the bunches and then to deliver them.' She also grew everlasting flowers from seeds she ordered from England, for large bouquets. 'It was quite fun for a while!' But after four or five years of persevering she surrendered to the demands of her garden because, as she said: 'It was being completely neglected.' Also, in the beginning, there were times when her husband had difficulties with his business. 'So I said: "Whatever happens the garden must go on. You mustn't sit and cry!" You can't believe, the garden . . . when something is wrong . . . you can't imagine!' She turned to us with an expression of bright-eyed animation. 'There is always something good in the garden!'

From March to November the garden flowers non-stop. There are veronicas of all kinds and campanulas, of which she has about twenty-five different ones grown from seed; fifteen varieties of salvias: 'This is a very nice sage from Germany. I love it. When the frost is on it, it is the nicest thing.' She grows four different kinds of bamboo: 'I wanted them just for the noise!' There are geraniums, agapanthus, columbines, bergamot and lilies. 'Daylilies I love! I have some very nice ones.' Parts of the garden are deliberately given over to subdued colours: to the sombre, chequered snake's-head fritillaries, to lavenders, including the dark purple, early-flowering French one, *L. stoechas*, which lasts all summer long, and there are fudge-coloured peonies as frail as tissue, containing gold stamens with crimson bases. Her peonies and irises are grown in a most imaginative way, not in clumps about the garden, but in a curving line of swooping colour so that when they are in bloom the effect is deliberately lengthened, yet when they are finished, the eye passes over the leaves to other plants in flower. To, for instance, the brazen effect of a psychedelic lime-yellow euphorbia, *E. polychroma*, lined up against the glare of a magenta 'Judas Tree' and the milder pink plumes of an aerial tamarisk.

Other shrubs and trees in the garden include kolkwitzias 'Bridal Wreath', hydrangeas, viburnums and magnolias, such as a lovely *M. wilsonii* with drooping white flowers full of crimson stamens, and the uncommon *Magnolia* x *watsonii* which can often look a bit out of sorts, though its creamy-white flowers give off such an overwhelming fragrance that you feel there must somewhere be a hidden source of healthy exuberance.

The garden is divided into specific areas, some of which flow one into the other, some of which are approached by four fine pergolas of generous width covered with a multitude of roses and clematis. One pergola leads to a serene area around a cast-iron bird table surrounded by the delicate cloudy grey of lavender planted along the edge of caramel-coloured rectangular paving. Another leads down to a shadowy secret garden entered by a barely disclosed iron gate. Here are snowdrops and early crocuses; violets, arabis,

Odile Masquelier grows her irises in long, wide curves.

potentillas, saxifrages, lady's mantle, tulips and hellebores against a background of *Choisya ternata*, viburnums and silver birches. The effect is so closely green and floral, smelling of dank earth and the underside of foliage, that you might be in the heart of some bosky hollow rather than on the brink of a city.

In the centre of the garden, below a deep pool overhung with a creamy 'Albéric Barbier' rose, is a sloping lawn which had once been a large meadow. 'I remember that my sister said you must dig it over, but we had just mowed, and were very young – with young children – and I was expecting my third. Instead we mowed it – very closely. And you see . . .' she gestured towards the dense green sward, 'but it was a very boring and insipid lawn!' To give the area some distinction and geometric formality Odile planted a double row of *Chamaecyparis lawsoniana* 'Columnaris' leading down to steps and to further rows of the conifers at right angles. 'I want to keep them thin, so they are very, very closely clipped. We have to take care when it snows to tie them securely.'

Discreetly hidden behind a low wall surrounded by a lethally prickly rose, 'Schneezwerg', to discourage children from climbing over, is her swimming pool. 'At the beginning I wanted no roses planted around the pool, so that I would not work in this part.' She threw out her hands, 'You see – in fact roses are coming. This is "Mermaid".' She gave us a humorous look, 'I think there *must* be a mermaid by the pool!' And then, because the wall to a small stone cottage on one side of the enclosure is so warm, she has planted against it the pretty convolvulus, *C. cneorum,* with pink buds opening to white, and a Moroccan broom, *Cytisus battandieri,* with yellow racemes smelling of pineapple.

The garden is run with streamlined efficiency and the help of various people including her housekeeper, someone to mow the grass and specialists to mend the tractor or build a wall. 'And last year I had students – marvellous students. One liked the garden so much he didn't go to the university! So then his mother called and said, "Listen, this can't go on." I said, "I'm sorry, I did nothing, you know." So they took him back to Paris!'

Pretty baskets are strategically placed for prunings; yards of hose-pipe circumnavigate the flower-beds; a ravening machine munches up bark for mulching and each rose, expertly tied-in and pruned, is labelled with its name, date, origin and family. Pots for just the right situation have been brought from as far away as Florence. There are both bold and hidden seats for every part of the garden; sculptures, such as triple faces carved in stone by Jean Granier and another by him of a woman washing her hair. Tiles, bricks and stones are brought into the garden from a variety of sources. 'I am reclaiming everything, you know – from a little derelict chapel came these stones. It is one of my pleasures!' But she finds it hard to get hold of cobbles. 'It's very difficult to get them from the city because they want to keep them for replacements! You really have to know someone on the spot.' She smiled, and looked a bit conspiratorial, 'We bought some . . .'

But if I am not getting the message over as to what sort of gardener owns this one hectare of land in the second largest city of France, a garden bursting at the seams and seething with innovation and dedicated plantsmanship, then that is because I have not yet really mentioned roses. Just to spell it out: Odile has between three and four hundred *different* roses. Long ago she gave up counting. And should anyone think her momentum might be flagging, when we were there she had just put in another seventy new varieties.

The majority of her roses come from André Eve at Pithiviers; others come from a rose grower in the Ardèche. Some are Bourbons such as the perfect cup-shaped 'Reine Victoria' and 'Louise Odier'; some are Damasks whose ancestry twines back to ancient times; others are Rugosas, varying from the well-known and fragile 'Frau Dagmar Hartop' to the more unusual amber and peppery lemon-scented 'Agnes'.

'All the Portland roses are here': those roses whose origins are confused and mysterious and which include the small 'Comte de Chambord' and the mottled 'Marbrée'. 'I have all these Pemberton roses,' said Odile – Hybrid Musks which were bred by the Rev. J. Pemberton early this century; roses such as a coppery-apricot 'Cornelia', 'Day Break', a musky rose with dense yellow buds opening to light sunlight, and 'Felicia' with sprays of silvery-pink fragrant flowers. 'They are darling, you know. They bloom, and bloom and bloom at least three times a year – until November. Sometimes at Christmas I can pick them.'

Among her Modern Shrub Roses are: 'Dentelle de Malines', 'Frühling-smorgen', 'Golden Wings' and 'The Fairy' – a small pink rose, useful for its habit of fitting in amongst more powerful flowers. Looking at a glossy-leafed pink rose groping between some flowers, Odile said, 'See, "Max Graf" mixed with all these people – makes such a wonderful tapestry in May.'

There are ramblers and climbers scrambling with clematis into trees, and up against the house and mixed with honeysuckle, that perfection of pure pinkness, 'Madame Grégoire Staechelin', whose shapely flowers dangle in the most maddening way so that she is difficult to see unless you stand beneath her.

In the garden are many species roses. One is an arching *Rosa willmottiae* which Odile says blooms for six weeks, others are a white *R.* 'Paulii' entangled with blue clematis 'Ramona' and 'Lasurstern', and that ravishing bright pink *R. californica plena* which looks so good in shadows and if given its head will sucker as avidly as speedwell sidles over grass.

Odile Masquelier is an indefatigable gardener. Her vitality, single-mindedness and knowledge seem boundless; her ambition is unwavering. But there are times when emotional susceptibility rather than abstraction, influence what Odile does in the garden. Rather self-mockingly she admitted that, 'Last year I planted "Thalie la Gentille" and "Pucelle de Lille" – just for their names!'

The serene garden on the upper level where the trees conceal a view of Lyon.

A GLIMPSE AT TWO GARDENS

I cannot cope with stalactites. Even less can I endure subterranean tours where the guide points out the similarity of these formations to Abraham Lincoln's profile. But I do love the Causses, where many of these grottoes are found, and I am not obliged to go underground. Yet.

The Causses are huge pieces of calcareous ground where waste and wilderness still exist after millions of years. Just to speak their names sends a shiver of awe down the spine – Causse de Sauveterre, Causse Noir, or the Causses du Gramat and Quercy. Up on this land mass, where winters are unendurable and an icy wind sweeps relentlessly across the endless limestone carapace, are abandoned villages of infinite desolation. Uninhabited ruins have immense charm. Someone once must have hewn the stone door-lintels and window ledges with patient perseverance, intending the houses to endure forever. Long ago shepherds made stone walls as they cleared the ground for sheep to graze the impoverished pastures. Now the stones lie among grass, and the junipers crouch in hideous deformities forever petrified by the prevailing wind. It is as hard to imagine the villages populated as it is to animate the great ruins of Mycenae. To visit the Causses, within a few miles of the river valleys of the Lot, Aveyron and Tarn heaving with fecundity in spring, is to experience a part of France at its extremes.

Just for a moment imagine taking flight from the Plomb du Cantal, 1855 metres high, and gliding southwards from the Auvergne, over the Causses, leaving the Rouergue to the west and the Cévennes to the east until you reach the tiny region of the Hérault, tucked behind the sweeping stretch of the Côte du Languedoc. A region of gorges and vineyards, of Douglas firs, spruces and terraces of sweet chestnuts and where the indigenous flower-pots have green or brown glaze arbitrarily trickling down their sides and the gardens have an uncontrived sense of form. It was here that we were making for, hoping to find village gardens, unsophisticated and pretty. We had no contacts and had made no assignations, but had been inveigled into the region by unformed memories of travellers' accounts of the Hérault.

The capital of the area is Clermont-l'Hérault, a small town specializing in military flags and seemingly full of spontaneous small gardens overflowing with *verveine* – those decorative verbenas of mauves and pinks oddly smelling of an English spring with their scent of primroses.

In the countryside, where plots of land were cultivated for modest crops, we saw an isolated cottage where roses grew through a vine shading a well, and where a few showy fat-headed peonies had strayed between a walnut and an apple tree. Somewhere else we walked through a hamlet, the kind of quiet place where there was no one about except for a woman carrying her granddaughter. Seeing us look over the wall into her garden, she beckoned us in. A straight gravel path led to the front door of her cottage, which was no taller than the surrounding, crooked fruit trees. Pink and crimson roses twined round the windows, and under a vine a cat lay sleeping on an iron table. She showed us her vegetables and her fruit bushes and named the aromatic plants which she and her husband had transplanted from the mountainside many years ago. They loved wild flowers, they loved the mountains and one day, when they were too infirm to walk on the mountains any longer, the garden would hold reminders of the *garrigues*: sages, thymes and marjoram; absinthe, grape hyacinth, cistus and lavender, with its conspicuous purple flowers used medicinally in ancient times and still laid among linen to keep away the moths, and the very decorative, spiny-headed blue globe thistle which when seen against the sun turns to a silver.

We lunched at Mourèze, a village of seventy-six inhabitants where the houses, with outside stairs, were threaded together by narrow alleyways and steps, and dominated by gigantic craggy rocks, contorted and grotesque. In the fading light at sunset black shadows appeared sensational and dramatic, in the early morning the lure of the rocks seemed irresistible, but Tamsin and I had to resist. The prospect of humping Cassandra round the convoluted *chemin des Charbonniers*, snaking between boulders, made us keep our heads. Instead we talked to an old man sitting on a wall in the sunlight. He told us there were many foreigners now living in the area; a German had bought a business and two houses. Another had bought a park. 'But here in our village the Germans aren't accepted, because of the past – we are always suspicious.' Elsewhere a whole village had been taken over by Belgians. And to our question as to how welcome were the foreigners, he said, 'That's an excellent question! If they integrate well, *pas de problème*, otherwise . . . ,' he shrugged, 'if they live like us, if they come and take the *pastis* with us at *midi* and play *boules* with us, we are like that.' And he raised two fingers together. 'The English, *bah!* – some integrate well.' But property is expensive, and the locals can no longer afford to buy. Then he added, his voice rising in exaggerated disbelief, '*Bof!* The English leave me their addresses, to be told when there's a plot of land or a house to sell. But,' he threw out his hands expressively, 'I'm not an agent!' We commiserated. 'Before,' he added regretfully, 'one thought one was travelling to a foreign country. But now – it's so *banal.*'

To the east of Mourèze, after crossing the Montpellier highway which leads north from Lodève to Millau where the empty road rises up over the magnificent Causse du Larzac, there is an area of vines. The fruity red wines of l'Hérault. It was hard to believe, having only just left the jagged fangs of the Mourèze, that within a few miles are sloping vineyards reminiscent of Alsace. We were going to a château, where the owner spoke of herself as being both French and British, having lived in France for thirty years. We had been given such a glowing recommendation as to the brilliance of her tiny terrace garden, by David Pugh the proprietor of 'Le Mimosa' at St-Guiraud, that we could not pass it up. Although we had not even eaten at his restaurant with its first-class reputation among travellers of many countries, David Pugh was kind enough to guide us to *le château d'Arboras.* Here Bouton Garrad and her husband Bill – both artists who hold a private exhibition in the château every other year – live among vineyards, distant horizons and vast skies.

Bouton Garrad described the soil which she copes with as null and void; good for vines but not for gardens. When the villagers saw the thymes and rosemarys she had planted among the stones, she said with laid-back good humour, 'They announced I was dotty!' Though roses are supposed to like this kind of clay, she finds the intense heat of summer far too much for them, except for one, a *Rosa banksiae alba-plena*, with lax tendrils of small white flowers, which seem to withstand the heat and flourish.

For such a small terrace standing above vines which lap like the sea along a shoreline, Bouton Garrad has a brilliant and esoteric collection of plants. Deciding on which plants to grow must require knowledge, ruthless selection, as well as a good deal of trial and error. 'I plant things that are a challenge.' One such plant is that benison of shrubs, the plumbago. Its wonderful blue remains cool and constant throughout the relentless drought of summer, never seeming to wilt, never needing much water. On the terrace, too, is a plant so alien to eyes conditioned to English gardens that it has a bizarre fascination. This is the *Aeonium arboreum foliis purpureis*, with fleshy leaves the shape of a rosette which, as the seasons move from winter to summer, change from green to a metallic purplish-black. Oddly, it is said to be used by Portuguese fishermen to harden their lines.

There is a datura with pendulous trumpet flowers and leaves tough as flannel, and against the walls are some really spectacular solanums: *S. jasminoides*, flowering all the summer in slate-blue clusters which bleach to white, *S. rantonnettii* with deep blue flowers, and *S. auranticum* with blue flowers and orange prickles. A self-clinging, evergreen *Trachelospermum jasminoides* with a sweetly dense fragrance from white flowers which mature to cream, is against the wall too, close to a less robust climber, *Mandevilla suaveolens*, the Chilean jasmine, its flowers like white periwinkles, and the cruel plant, *Araujia sericofera*, with grooved pods full of silky seeds and sweet-scented white flowers whose glutinous pollen traps moths, keeping them captive till daylight.

'For me, this is the grandmother and grandfather of all citrus fruit,' Bouton said of her *Poncirus trifoliata* (Japanese bitter orange). It is a shrub with apple-green leaves, sweetly-scented white flowers and miniature globular green fruit ripening to yellow. It also has the most vicious two-and-a-half-inch spines.

As for her 'lawn' – it is unique. 'I have a hatred of green – so I try to avoid it!' Quite a handicap for a gardener, you would think. But with great ingenuity, and resulting in something so pretty, Bouton has overcome her aversion by planting a small patch of blue *Verbena tenera*. 'All the French who come, say, "*Oh, c'est un jardin anglais.*" At first I couldn't think what they were talking about. What they meant was – it's a mess!'

Off the terrace and to one side of the château is a swimming pool. Around it grows a pretty purple lavender with narrow, serrated leaves, *Lavandula dentata*, which most agreeably flowers all the year round. Nearby is a small vegetable garden. 'We only grow things that are difficult to find in the shops. We usually keep one of everything.' She also buys aubergines grafted onto tomato plants. 'They ripen much sooner than ordinary aubergines. I only need two plants – they produce an enormous crop.' Cats darted about, dodging round the Cape gooseberries and raspberries, a misunderstood fruit according to Bouton. 'It's a myth that raspberries don't like heat, but they need lots of water.'

She pointed to some elegant edible thistles. 'Look! There's cardoon – they're very decorative – a first cousin to the globe artichoke. It's the stems one eats – but they're pretty horrible, actually!' A close relative to the cardoon is *Carlina acaulis*, a low-growing thistle with shiny, papery bracts which, curiously, we had seen pinned to doors as we crossed the mountains of the Massif Central. We were most intrigued; they looked ornamental – all silvery and brittle – but why on doors? Found above the tree-line, they are gathered, we were told, to bring good luck to the household.

The next garden could hardly have been more different. It was the *Parc Floral des Moutiers* at Varengeville near Dieppe, belonging to the Mallet family. I write about it briefly in this section, *Jardins Raffinés*, not for the garden which is well-known and open to the public, but because Madame Mallet, the owner, was so responsive, articulate and helpful with advice on gardens all over the country. She also had spirited views on the French, and on gardening in general.

Owing to Guillaume Mallet's admiration for English gardens when he bought *Les Moutiers* in 1898, the enlargement of the house and the construction of surrounding walled enclosures were designed for him by Edwin Lutyens, while the original garden was laid out by Gertrude Jekyll. The large park, full of groves and springs as well as fine trees and flowers, contains a magnificent collection of azaleas and rhododendrons and a strong residue of William Robinson's intuition for 'the placing of perfectly hardy exotic plants in places where they will take care of themselves'.

Guillaume Mallet's delicate eye and impressionable susceptibilities provoked him into using pieces of damask, brocade and velvet as a guide to creating the colours of the Renaissance among his flowering shrubs. If they turned out to be the wrong colours he would plant and replant until he achieved the effect, from flowers, of a medieval stained-glass window. Such refinement among the rhododendrons remains visible today.

We had actually come to *Les Moutiers* looking for Robert Mallet. At Courson, where we had briefly met, he said he could help us; he could give us garden addresses. But on arrival at his *Centre d'Art Floral* next door to his mother's manor house, *Les Moutiers*, we received only a negative shrug. 'Where is Robert?' seemed to be the universal cry in Mallet territory. No one knew. And that is how we found ourselves walking across the grass towards the garden and the Lutyens house where, quite fortuitously, we had a chance encounter with the remarkable Madame Mallet.

She responded with immediate warmth, and having been involved in the early beginnings of Courson, she had opinions on other flower shows. 'Showing a plant without being able to buy it, is terribly sadistic!' was her pithy comment. And how to avoid the vulgarity of these other, more famous events? 'Courson keeps its freshness because we are very careful continually to introduce new, young people. It's a supermarket of rare plants.' She added fervently, 'And I will fight for its life – even if I have to wear a bullet-proof jacket!'

Although she was expecting to take a party of tourists around the garden at any moment, she said in fluent English, 'Quick! Come in, and I'll just show you round the house before I have a group.' She took my arm and added, effusively, 'I'm always having groups.' We hurried through the house, grabbing visually at the Arts and Crafts details of texture and design, perspective and materials, while she talked about the place. 'I love the ghosts here! The house is full of ghosts.' We stood in the drawing-room looking out on the finely designed landscape as she went on, 'Well – I was certainly the first to open my garden in France. The very first. And I remember Charles de Noailles [the creator of the famous garden near Grasse] saying, "Well, now! It can be done!" But I said, I don't want any publicity. I have no posters. I have nothing. I make no profit. I just want people to go round.

'All the Belgians, all the Dutch, all the English, and now the Americans – they come to see. And old ladies of my age come – in groups. And in the last three years we have had the state schools. I receive them myself!' She leant towards me, grasping my arm impulsively. 'Usually children aren't allowed on the grass. But I allow it – and they love it! I know how to talk to children.' She scorns the number of French people who look at *Le Parc Floral des Moutiers* as merely a possession. 'They can't get it out of their heads. They say, "*Oh, là, là*. It is money." The French haven't changed their mentality!' They annoy her further when they ask if she has children to inherit the place. 'I tell them – of course I have children. But it isn't because I have children that I maintain the garden!' Emphatically she added, 'You can't inherit any more. It is finished. I mean – nowadays children have to earn their living!'

Outside again, waiting for her group to arrive, Madame Mallet spoke with intensity. 'We had two wars on our land. We didn't have time to garden. It was impossible!' We were standing at the foot of the front steps where there were long-established deep flower-beds either side of the wide path leading away from the house; the borders looked Jekyllish and there was a strong scent of England. 'It was before 1917 that all the beautiful gardens were made, you see. Since then, I don't know what happened, but from 1940 to 1955 people only had time to rebuild their houses.' And then, standing among her climbers, arbours, flower borders, Lutyens' legacies, and facing an approaching party of eager foreigners, she said, 'A garden can't live very long – you can't imagine it will remain. But if it is a time of beauty, and it gives beauty, then that beauty will go somewhere else.' Like an impassive portent her voice continued, 'I don't know where – it's of no importance, no importance at all.' And she vanished into a crowd of colourful tourists who surely would clash badly with Renaissance brocade.

PLANTS FROM ALL
FIVE CONTINENTS

'*Pour m'appeler dans le jardin sonnez la cloche.*' The notice was propped up against a large hand-bell on the ground. The garden belonged to Brigitte Fourier whom we had been introduced to briefly at Courson in May, and who had willingly agreed to our request to visit her. We knew even before we walked through the gates that we were going to see a garden of great distinction. In close horticultural circles she was reputed to be a most knowledgeable and discriminating gardener. Although she lived in a village, I had somehow imagined her being on the outskirts, but what we found was a true village garden, large and walled, on an out-of-the-way headland reaching into the Golfe du Morbihan, a strange land-locked sea where the Atlantic pours in through a gap only six hundred metres wide, creating a tidal flow of some sixteen feet. Here the light seemed to be more transparent than anywhere I had seen.

This was southern Brittany. 'The country was wild and the language unknown to me, the natives were brutal and barbarous . . .' wrote Pierre Abélard, about eight hundred years before we arrived. Abélard, having been persecuted and brutally castrated for his love affair with Héloïse, fled from Paris and took refuge in the monastery at St-Gildas-de-Rhuys, Morbihan. There he became Abbot until the conniving monks, attempting to poison him, finally drove Abélard to escape and find shelter in distant Cluny. He died there in 1142. But his love letters to Heloïse, and hers to him, remain a classic legacy of their tragic separation.

Our experiences were different. Barbarity was far from evident in the countryside, where the stone houses have slate roofs and handsome stone lintels to the windows. Some of the town houses have protective laurel hedges, thick and gloomy in the small, iron-railed front gardens. On rainy days the downstairs rooms must be Stygian though the laurels are preferable, perhaps, to the 'frosted' conifers prevalent in other parts of France. There was nothing barbaric or wild about the sight of an old man in a faded blue cotton jacket buying his *viande* from the travelling shop; the only threatening moment was in a village *boucherie* when the butcher's wife, looking at Cassandra, remarked 'What plump little legs. Just feel!'

The transparent light of the Morbihan.

We had arranged with Madame Fourier to arrive in the afternoon. Having entered through green gates set in the ancient stone wall surrounding the garden, and rung the bell as instructed, we were welcomed by a lady dressed in the most perfect gardening gear I have ever seen. Knee-length shorts, indestructible shoes, a small canvas hat and best of all, her waistcoat. This was a garment made for the *chasse*, a hunting jacket that the French, who view the killing of all forms of wildlife as almost a ritualistic activity, design with such imagination. Pockets abound. There was not a fraction of space wasted into which the hunter could not stuff his cartridges, knife, cigarettes, bottle of *marc* or dead carcasses. How far less belligerent to fill them with secateurs, pruning knife and gloves, with plant ties and raffia. It was a paragon of gardening jackets, and I envied Madame Fourier instantly.

Her house, built about a hundred years ago, was fine and sturdy; Brigitte Fourier described it as a master mariner's house. 'So *agréable*. I love life going on around me. One has the noise, of course, and there are a lot of inconveniences. One's always fighting against electric wires and then, you know, we have houses suddenly coming up like mushrooms.'

Monsieur and Madame Fourier bought the house twenty-two years ago when the village was very small. Since then a little port has been built and tourism here, like everywhere else, has bounded ahead, though fortunately the season only lasts for about three months. From an upstairs room, painted serenely white, is an unblemished view of her garden, the trees, the sea and little boats.

The temperate Breton climate allows Brigitte Fourier to grow plants from all five continents. The springs are usually docile, summers are moderate with occasional showers, autumns are wet and followed by mild winters, except when high gales slam relentlessly along the coasts, making the seas mountainous and spectacular and drifting the salt-laden air far inland.

Around the house, which stands on a mound with views towards the *Golfe du Morbihan*, the garden slopes gently down towards the sea. The more cultivated part of the garden covers about one hectare, but the informal part, furthest from the house, amounts to roughly two. Brigitte Fourier has contrived distinct areas, one hidden from the other by hedges of hornbeam, '*plein de poésie et de secrets*', so that there is a feeling of calm security about the whole domain. Nowhere is exposed or challenging; it has a tranquil atmosphere where you pause and saunter, knowing as you move on that there will be further comfort the other side of the hedge.

Madame Fourier's mastery of gardening germinated long ago. Not in gardens, but in a school for Decorative Arts. 'Architecture, sculpture, painting – I loved it!' She spoke with a kind of resignation as she added, '. . . but I find that, how to say it? . . . I prefer to work with plants, with the earth.' Every gardener is tactile, but Brigitte Fourier is quietly demonstrative as she touches leaves or bends to kiss some plant that has responded to her solicitude. She points to a *Macleaya cordata* which, after her tender cherishing, has grown into tall plumes of pearly-white. 'In winter it vanishes back to nothing.' For the difficult month of August she grows Japanese anemones – those lovely unassuming flowers, either white as china or the pink of chilled hands, which, once established, can be relied upon to lubricate the parched dullness of a late summer garden. Roses and clematis twine luxuriantly. A 'Mermaid' rose with fat buds on the point of opening mingles with the clematis 'Niobe', the deep red of crimson velvet; there are ceanothus, philadelphus and a diversity of myrtles. Among her many camellias is 'Cornish Snow' – not the white one, but the clone 'Winton', the dusky pink of almond blossom. If the weather becomes very cold this winter it will die, for Madame Fourier explains they are gardening at the limit, and three bitter winters followed by two hot summers have been catastrophic. Yet gardens are always compensating their gardeners. Disasters throw up alternatives, whether it is the destruction of trees which opens up an unexpected view, or the death of something precious being replaced by something much more meritorious.

Among the kalmias, rhododendrons, azaleas and white flowering escallonias are pittosporums. One in particular is outstanding, *Pittosporum tobira*, a large shrub from Japan with creamy flowers smelling of orange-blossom. Bushy salvias of an inimitable blue, from the Canary Islands, fragile romneya, hellebores, hibiscus which perversely seem to do well without much sunlight, and daylilies, are all to be found in the garden along with her beautiful sorrel tree, *Oxydendrum arboreum*, needing lime-free soil but agreeable to either shade or sun, which turns to a flaunting brilliance of crimson and yellow in autumn.

Her garden evolved slowly, bit by bit. 'When I get a plant I spend a lot of time deciding where I'm going to put it. So I walk around cradling the plant and very often I change its placing several times. I correct, I modify. For me a garden is never finished.' She barely ever sprays; if a plant is sick she either cuts it right back or is ruthless and throws it out. She has no ambition whatsoever to be competitive or for her garden to appear pushy or assertive; all she wants is that it should integrate into the character of the Breton countryside. As she quietly said, 'No one sees that there are extraordinary plants here – only I know.' And as if to emphasise her words, she shows me a camellia in a secluded part of the garden. 'It's very pretty. No one sees it. But I love it.'

Even the personal names for different parts of the garden are homely and unpretentious. One is called '*la dame gentille*', after a very kind neighbour; another, in the direction of a farm raising guinea fowl, is '*les pintades*'; one of her neighbours is a baker, so the nearby garden is '*le boulanger*'; '*le pré du puits*' is a meadow with a well in it, and one of her granddaughters, the same age as some of the trees they planted eight years ago, was the inspiration for '*le bois de Charlotte*'.

Because her botanical knowledge is so extensive and because Madame Fourier has an enquiring and academic approach as well as an emotional one, her taste is robust and decisive. She speaks critically of weeping plants, whether they be trees or shrubs, but is ardently committed to the polarity of large plants growing among small ones. She is also an experimenter; trying to break away from what is accepted planting, to free herself from current trends. The vogue for blue and white gardens which '. . . you more or less see everywhere', she disregards. 'One has to find one's own personal approach, I believe.' In a little space which was once a yellow and white garden and then became solely white, she is once more experimenting with her original scheme. Her mood is different, her spirits are jaunty, perhaps she will keep it this way. 'In the end I like it – yellow and white – it's gay. Very gay!'

Mature pine trees were well established when the Fouriers first began to make the garden. In these trees Brigitte Fourier has the billowing climbing rose 'Wedding Day', with trusses of white flowers smelling of oranges, and one of its parents, *Rosa sinowilsonii*, thrusting their insinuating tendrils far into the darkness overhead. The effect is overwhelming and mysterious.

Speak about trees to Brigitte Fourier and her eyes light up with devotion. Throwing her arms around a tree trunk she admits that though some of her little gardens are too shady, the idea of felling any trees for the sake of sunlight appals her.

Trees are deeply rooted in Madame Fourier's heart as well as in the earth; they are essential to her garden. Among her collection of about fifteen magnolias is a *Magnolia delavayi* with parchment-white flowers and massive leaves the colour of the sea, *M. grandiflora* 'Samuel Sommer' with fragrant ivory flowers fourteen inches in diameter and leaves which charmingly form bouquets at the end of the branches, and a *M.* x *veitchii* with blush-pink flowers appearing on the naked twigs.

Through a wooden gate leading into a field is a magnificent collection of more than twenty alders. 'They grow quickly and seem to like it here

Trees, their form, foliage and shadows, are Brigitte Fourier's first love.

whether they come from Formosa, Manchuria or Japan.' From southern Europe grows the conical-shaped *Alnus cordata,* and another, *A. crema-stogyne*, is a tree which has been known to reach eighty feet, according to Ernest Henry Wilson who discovered it in Szechuan, China, almost a hundred years ago. She loves this tree in particular for its *très beau tronc*'. In the same meadow are two of her most precious trees which she bought in Holland, *Emmenopterys henryi*. They are rare deciduous beauties from China with bronze shoots in spring. When they are mature enough to bloom they will flaunt pyramidal corymbs of large white flowers. Among her willows is a *recherché* salix, originating in the wadis of the Atlas mountains, which she received from the arboretum of Roger de Vemorin at Verrières.

Her collection of evergreens is important and so comprehensive it is impossible to name them all. But some of her beloved ones, which she describes as *'impeccable'*, include two small trees, *Ilex rotunda* from Japan, and *I. perado platyphylla* from the Azores, with distinctly broad leaves all dark green and leathery. 'I like this,' she said, pointing to a New Zealand *Podocarpus totara*, 'because one doesn't think it's a conifer! It's a little yellow, it pricks a bit, it may be rather delicate – but not too much and sometimes I give it *une bonne coupe*!' There are handsome evergreen oaks, *Quercus ilex*, with toothed, dark glossy leaves and a pendulous demeanour. From Japan she once brought back a tender evergreen *Cinnamomum japonicum* which she honours for having a *'rustique'* personality, and she has a distinguished silvery box, *Buxus sempervirens 'Elegantissima'*. There is a most beautiful shrub with cinnamon-red bark, *Arbutus* x *andrachnoides*, and *Euonymus japonicus* which copes with either sun or shade; sweet-smelling *Osmanthus heterophyllus*; a holly-leaved cherry, *Prunus ilicifolia*, which comes from California and in summer has racemes of white flowers followed by red berries which turn purply-black. Other evergreens include a collection of the slow-growing family of *Raphiolepis*, some of which are found in the Midi, some from as far away as Japan, Korea and China; and it was from China that her husband brought back a most superb hybrid azalea, 'Satsuki', pink, with showy dark blotches.

It is the survival of these evergreens, whether they come from the southern or the northern hemisphere, that perpetually intrigues Brigitte Fourier. She meticulously notes their origins, wanting to know what country, what climate they come from, at the same time marvelling how well they integrate now that they have become Breton. As she puts it: *'Ces plantes sont devenues bretonnes, elles se sont fondues dans le paysage.'*

This large village garden, walled, private and full of trees and secrecy, is not Madame Fourier's only concern. There is also her husband's garden. It is his entirely, although she helped him with the original design which was based on a plan for a garden of the early nineteenth century, now hanging in the hall. Now she only advises and encourages him.

This garden is enchanting. It is small, atmospheric and very formal and it lies a few hundred metres from their house. Surrounded by walls on three sides, yet not so high as to hide a neighbouring orchard of old fruit trees, and lying behind a cottage where the children come to stay, the garden is entirely green and geometric. A contorted fig tree, a magnificent mulberry and an olive tree are the only deviant shapes, except for small ferns in steps and walls ruffling up the shadows. Old weathered paving stones, a bay tree cut into three tiers, and the funereal colours from hellebores still in flower give a sombre appearance of immense repose. Returning through the village to her house, Madame Fourier admitted that her garden is at its best from mid-April to mid-June, but her husband's garden is undeniably impressive in winter.

Listening to Brigitte Fourier talk about her garden it is hard to fathom her inherent feelings towards it. There are layers of response which at first seem to be contradictory; but later, on reflection, I decided that she was accounting for the way gardens draw out of you a diversity of reactions. Some are facile, lightweight yet very personal; others can be so profound, so instinctive that you are hardly aware of the garden's tenacity. Brigitte Fourier seemed to be a gardener in whom all these contrary feelings were vibrating. She did not have the single-minded pursuit of Anne Simonet with her love for scents, or the brothers Jean and Paul with their perpetual quest for exotics. Instead she was almost a captive to the whim of the garden, and yet her profound knowledge of plants kept her control steadfast.

But this is not the end. There are few legacies for future generations as noble as trees. Brigitte Fourier's allegiance to them is so intemperate that she and her husband have now decided to plant trees on another two hectares of their land. The enticement is compelling. She finds it wildly invigorating and challenging to be working on such a large scale where she will no longer be constrained by walls. Since they started to plant trees into the landscape, Madame Fourier admits that their lives have changed.

'WE'VE HAD GARDENERS
FOR UMPTEEN YEARS'

There are sad gardens in France where the splendour of other eras has slowly been eroded by the passing generations. They have such poignancy and are so integral to this collection of French gardens that these places cannot be shrugged off as 'has-beens'. Their owners struggle, pouring devotion and energy into what is happening under their feet, while looking back to a heritage when their ancestors, with boundless resources, first created their estates.

I have to admit an especial love towards these gardens. The melancholy, the stone carvings worn away by seasons of rainfall, the boldness of topiary first conceived when pruners were two-a-penny, and the gallant spirit of the present-day owners who have had to come to terms with mediocrity and who yet carry on with a certain panache. Foisted as they are with an onerous garden legacy, their resolve is still buoyed up by some inner fervour. I take off my hat to their tenacity, for I know that with their departure will have gone the last residue, the last shadow of the past. At present, like frail skeletons of leaves, these properties are still held intact by their owners. We will not lament, but we should pay homage.

One such is the Marquise de Beauregard. There is nothing sentimental or self-pitying about her. She is warm-hearted, sardonic, acerbic and indomitable. And she is treading water vigorously to keep her château and its estate afloat. When I spoke to her from England she was responsive and welcoming; in elegant English she immediately asked us for lunch and apologized for not having us to stay, explaining that she had not yet moved out of her winter quarters.

On a spring day of pellucid light with hedges full of hawthorn blossom and fields full of buttercups we turned east for the Lake of Geneva. *En route* we wanted to look at a monastery *potager* on the outskirts of Bourg-en-Bresse at Brou. The church at Brou is a masterpiece, but its vibrations are personal and tragic, and impossible to shake off once you have learnt its history. In 1480 Marguerite de Bourbon made a vow to transform the humble priory at Brou into an abbey if her prayers were answered and her husband, Philippe, Comte de Bresse, who was paralysed from a hunting

PREVIOUS PAGE
Flowers for the house.

accident, was restored to health. He was, but alas she died so soon after, that it was not until 1504 that her daughter-in-law, mourning the death of her own young husband, fulfilled Marguerite's vow.

Within the church are three tombs. The effigies of Marguerite, her son Philibert le Beau and her daughter-in-law, with their embroidered pillow, dog and lion, their tranquil countenances forever petrified in Carrara marble, are so touchingly portrayed you envy them their serene immortality.

But what we had come to find was the monastery with the Musée de l'Ain now housed upstairs in three of its rooms. From here I was hoping to get a bird's eye view of a complex design of well-controlled fruit trees, herbs and vegetables which, perhaps, had changed little over several hundred years. Unfortunately our late arrival left us a scant twenty minutes before the museum would close for two hours, but the doorman proved, miraculously, to belong to that unusual breed of kindly custodians and, seeing our desperate and breathless condition, waved us in.

We might not have troubled. What was spread beneath us as we peered through tall windows was the final withering of past refinement. Like everything, lack of money and changing values had reduced the monks' garden to a forlorn travesty.

Thirty years ago, for reasons of easy maintenance, the garden had been divided into a number of large squares. No one wanted to take on its upkeep so it was left to the keepers of the museum. 'Any of us could garden there. I gave up mine two years ago,' the concierge said, obviously chagrined that we had come all this way to his museum only to be disappointed. As a final justification, as a small nugget of philosophical comfort for what had happened to the *potager*, he threw out his hands: 'You must always run nowadays, you understand? We had only two days off a week.' As we turned to leave he called out to us, 'And sometimes it rained on one of them.'

Skirting Geneva we passed concrete basins of mauve and orange pansies interspersed with blocks of cream, blue and yellow beds dividing groups of *Rosa scabrosa* in force-ten pink. Gentler to the eyes was the sight of hang-gliders from Mont Salève drifting like white and rosy petals in the humid down-draughts high above the escarpment. This is a part of France I find hard to take seriously. Somehow, I think, Switzerland on its northern shore has seeped south and diluted Gallic verve with the deadly hand of order, time-keeping, and of course adherence to doors marked Exit. This is very subjective. And it rankles; for many times I have been accosted by a public-spirited Swiss who has ticked me off for using the wrong entrance;

for parking on the wrong side of the street; and once – oh impropriety, oh trangression! – for opening a map on the bonnet of his car.

The first impression on arriving at the Château de Beauregard on the shores of Lac Léman is of birdsong. In May the towering and ancient trees surrounding the château are full of birds, unseen but vocal, filling the foliage with such a resonance of song it caused us to walk with our heads thrown back looking for the source.

The château, which goes back to 1270, has an almost fictional lineage. Before 1690 when the Costa family acquired it, it had belonged to the marquise's own ancestors. 'Very romantic!' the marquise declared. But now that she is a widow, after more than sixty years of marriage, the marquise travels much of the year or spends some months of the winter in Lausanne. A couple look after the place in her absence, though during the summer she employs an additional two cooks. 'We are at least twenty-five in the house,' the marquise explained, 'without speaking of the servants.'

The eighty-four-year old marquise, very upright and walking with an agile step, has brilliant blue eyes which do not miss a thing. 'I have a slave who does part of the kitchen garden,' she announced as she led the way towards the walled *potager*. 'We don't have a gardener living in any more because I've had too much trouble with Social Security. In France you are asked, does this gardener plant carrots? *Bon*! Does he pick them too, or someone else? I exaggerate a bit,' she makes a mocking grimace, 'but at the end of the month there was always a fight as to what category he was in!'

In the warm air the scent of box from the small hedges surrounding formal enclosures rose all around us. 'We've had gardeners for umpteen years – but when they died we got a new generation who do their eight hours and not a second more.' She spoke with scathing sarcasm, remembering times before the war when gardeners were loyal and dedicated. Parsley, rhubarb, sweet williams, raspberries, ('they are indispensable!') and a colourful collection of salads showed that part of the ancient *potager* was still cherished. But the old fruit trees, which added a buckled beauty to the overall effect, were long past their best and the vines were neglected. 'They are no good. They get diseases and it isn't worth the trouble.' Yet looking at the ghostly patterns where once the paths had been regularly raked it was possible to sense how, not so long ago, the garden had been a place of order and symmetry where an abundance of fruit and vegetables had supplied the house with a continual stream of lavish nourishment.

'I don't say I'm letting it go, but the fruit trees are too much work.

With Lac Léman in the distance the garden at Beauregard, with its topiary and gravel paths, epitomizes French gardens.

Anyway, the children will do what they want. They know nothing about it
– they're not interested. None of them!' The marquise spoke tersely. Then
with resignation she added, 'They say, "Oh, it's all right, Mummy likes the
garden. Granny likes the garden." It's very nice for them to come and get
flowers when they need them – but that's all.' She picks some dead petals
off an iris. 'They wouldn't think of doing this as they pass!'

Her collection of irises was dynamic. There were reds, dark as glossy
chenille, and so rich and opulent in that setting they gave an appearance of
alien nonconformity. There were yellows as fluorescent as gold-leaf, and
blues with the density of fur. Others were of colours so aberrant they had
the hue of old bruises. 'I have eighteen varieties. I get them from a nursery
behind Rolle, higher than I am.' She waved in a north-easterly direction,
across the lake towards Switzerland. 'They sell all over the world.'

She introduced us to her gardener, as enthusiastic and energetic as
herself: 'Ten years I've had my gardener, Monsieur Martin. We've fought a
lot! We have great discussions,' the marquise said as we walked towards the
farm buildings forming part of the courtyard, 'and he's always right, of
course!' A sporadic chime of cow-bells could be heard nearby, a sound I had
not expected at lake-level in France. The marquise explained: 'Those cows
don't have milk yet – I don't know what you call them. Yes, heifers. Well,
the heifers go up to the mountains for summer. They'll be going shortly.'

Once, Monsieur Martin told us, there had been two mandarin trees in
pots at each of the five barn doors. Ten trees! How the effect must have
added shapely elegance to the courtyard. Sadly, though, in spite of
bringing the trees inside each winter, unexpected frosts had reduced them
to four. Slowly, so slowly the old practices were being usurped, and each
time, as some other long-standing tradition caved in despite the marquise's
gallant efforts to keep the place together, the imperceptible decline took
another relentless step. As she admitted, 'Tulips and narcissus – I never put
fresh ones in now, because half the time I'm not here.'

As we walked round with the marquise and her gardener, they kept up a
sparring commentary on everything we looked at. Asked about trimming
the box and yew hedges and pyramids, the marquise gave a derisive hoot
while Monsieur Martin admitted that the day before they had argued.
'Madame wants them cut very early in the season. I don't!' (A familiar
dilemma to every gardener threatened by frost.) Showing us a bed of
impatiens he pointed out, 'I'd rather change this, but . . .' and he shrugged
his shoulders, 'it belongs to madame la marquise.' When arranging pots of
them in the courtyard: 'Madame wants some white and pink, with a few
red.' 'I like that mixture,' snapped the marquise. 'Well, I don't know . . .'

Monsieur Martin said cryptically, 'and some people don't approve.'

At the back of the château is an almost perpendicular drop from the terrace to a sweep of grass to the water's edge where ducks were nudging at the bank, and swans were floating alongside their reflections. Around the curious five-sided twelfth-century tower we could hear the crusty caw of rooks being blown about the sky like scraps of torn plastic. It was Sunday; from across the lake came the distant sound of church bells. The marquise pointed to the lake, 'Well, I promise you it gives us enough bother. Someone is always trying to land on our lake shore. You can't imagine! They come by boat and we are invaded.' Her memory goes back to years of seclusion, when the countryside was pastoral. 'You see how it's built all over? It's a disaster! Here we're becoming a suburb of Geneva. As for Yvoire, it's a most ghastly village. You know St Paul de Vence? Well, it's ten times worse! Ghastly! Ghastly!'

The *Jardin du Midi*, where we went to have drinks before lunch, is strictly formal and unequivocally French. The surrounding low box hedges are cut into crenellations, gravel paths divide the four quarters of lawn, which are edged by forty-two standard roses with decorative pink heads and not a hair out of place. Clipped yew pyramids are precisely placed to make emphatic verticals casting black shadows on the chaste grass. In the centre, around a massive stone urn, is a circular bed divided into segments of golden marigolds and blue ageratums. 'Blue and yellow, always,' the marquise told us.

One of the most startling sights in the garden is the bed of agapanthus. 'The agapanthus are huge,' the marquise said, 'one year we had a hundred and seventy-five! Now there are around eighty to a hundred.' Then she added as though stating the obvious, 'I count them every day – so nobody can pinch some.'

A stone seat of the last century, covered with moss and with a patina like map tracings, contrasts with a group of bold wooden chairs and a table, in strong yellow, nicely picking up the yellows of the flowers in the central bed. 'We brought them back from Portugal in 1936 because we hated the normal ghastly garden furniture!' In most gardens such an aggressive chrome would eclipse everything else, but in this part of the garden, with deep variegations of greens, with the castle walls the cool colours of heterogeneous stone and shutters of faded ox-blood, the furniture standing in deep shadows looked stunning.

'If you don't like the lunch, blame my cook!' the marquise warned us as we walked towards her winter quarters. 'I never do the cooking.' We were served with a most exquisite lunch, including that classic dish, *blanquette de veau*; polenta quite unlike the solid wedges Tamsin and I had previously tasted ('plenty of butter, plenty of milk,' Georgina, who was serving at table, told us); and green salad from the *potager*. 'None of us need cheese!' the marquise declared as Georgina appeared with a tart of wild strawberries piled on pastry as light as dissolving snow.

One of the charms of the two hundred acres of the Beauregard estate is the wood. Through large wrought-iron gates is a wide path flanked by banks of periwinkles, hellebores, primroses and lilies-of-the-valley. Meandering off this central track are paths twining through the trees where the tall canopy of foliage is so dense the forest is mysteriously stealthy.

On the edge of the wood is a Wellingtonia planted a hundred and fifty years ago when it was fashionable to put in these stately trees. The marquise's tree is a giant; its tapering trunk of reddish-grey bark, which when you knock it has a sort of internal resonance like a sepulchral voice, soars to an incredible height. The Wellingtonia is one of the oldest living things in the world and has been discovered to live for about four thousand years. That should comfort the marquise. And the tulip tree . . . Its Latin name is so beautiful I must write it here, *Liriodendron tulipifera*. (God knows where the stresses really come, but the way I say it to myself it lilts along.) What a tree, with its open crown and distinctive leaves which look as though someone had taken a bite out of each one. This specimen was the best I had ever seen, even though its greenish-white flowers, looking more like water-lilies than tulips, were not yet in bloom. In autumn the tree turns yellow – a pure cadmium colour so that when the leaves scatter the ground, it seems from a distance as though a crop of sternbergias had miraculously appeared overnight.

In this part of the estate too, along the lakeside, are oak trees planted before the French Revolution. 'I tell you,' the marquise said, 'we still have papers – documents – to say when they were planted. Those down there are over two hundred years old. There are only four left. See how they are leaning over the water.' Then she added with a sudden heartfelt resignation, 'Everything needs continual attention.' That summer she was having the château roof repaired. 'I am making an effort because I think, one day, this place has got to survive.' Her spirit was undaunted. 'I want to leave it in good condition. My children won't have the energy to keep this place up.' Then with a conspiratorial smile she said, 'I mow the grass when they're around. It gives my family awful remorse to see me at it! They lie in the sun – and it upsets them . . .' Her voice became inaudible as a sudden sound like the beat of horses' hoofs filled the air, and three swans rose from the lake and with necks outstretched flew towards the coast of Switzerland.

Returning to the garden from the wood full of wild flowers.

HALF-TRANCED ON WINE
AND SENSUALITY

Colonel Challan Belval's garden is the antithesis of the marquise's at Beauregard. Here dereliction has already taken over. As with the Parthenon or the ruins of Ankhor-Wat, the patina of decay, the slow years of metamorphosis, have turned the place into something atmospheric and poignant. What we see now is far removed from its origins centuries ago.

The garden at Moutier Saint-Jean, near Dijon, has such palpable *tristesse*, and such an ephemeral handhold on life as it lapses year after year into poetic dilapidation, that it brings a lump to the throat. We may never have known its days of past grandeur but, like looking through the scrim on a stage set, we cannot help being aware of other shapes when the garden was radiant and fair. Listening to the present descendant speak of ancient splendours, it is still possible to become enthralled.

The garden forms part of the property where a family with the legendary title of Coeur-de-Roy, have lived since 1556. As members of the judiciary, as reformers, founders of hospitals and men of letters, the family has a distinguished pedigree. In 1683, at the age of fifty-six, Jean Coeur-de-Roy, President of the *parlement* at Dijon, came to live permanently at the family home of Moutier Saint-Jean; here he held a kind of regional royal court where his decisions never seem to have been contested. An austere and private man, he had the imagination to lay out the garden whose traces we still see today and whose fountains and fishponds were the envy of the Auxois.

There are two levels to the property; the upper one is approached through the first of eight gateways (number 5 on the plan) onto a tribune, or raised platform, edged by a row of obelisks from where one can look down onto the walled garden in the shape of an apse. At either end of the tribune flights of stone steps, beside the 'blind' gateways two and three (6 & 7), lead down to an area almost given over to coarse grass, where a few roses and espaliers do still decorate the walls. At the far end of the apse there are identical seventeenth-century '*portes*' (1 & 2) each side of the sixth (3), an impressive central gateway embellished with curlicues and three stone balls.

The garden on the lower level has a double flight of steps either side of a vaulted grotto, a nymphaeum, where a seventh (8) superb entrance leads out of the grotto along the main pathway to the eighth (4) gate at the far end, containing a stone bench.

Within these two imposing enclosures is romantic confusion and wilderness; the grass is rank, the wild flowers proliferate and there is a general air of sunburnt decadence where things fall apart and the centre can no longer hold. Yet walking slowly in sunlight, hearing the constant whine of insects, it is possible to feel the impulse and spirited imagination which the garden designers, inspired by the renowned sixteenth-century architects Philibert de L'Orme and Sebastiano Serlio, first brought to their imposing layout. Using six different designs, the eight gateways were built with alternating blocks of faced limestone and lumps of pitted and porous chalky rock. This weird tufa comes from the Forêt de Morcon only fifteen kilometres from the village. The design has the quality of fairy stories; an unreality hangs about a place where four of the majestic portals lead nowhere: their charm is that through them you can walk off into the parched fields.

Eroded and weathered as the eight monumental gateways are, with a leap of the imagination we can sharpen their outlines, resurrect the finials, mend the scrolls, restore the bull's-eye, repair the classical pediments, replace the stone *boules* and dress the garden with *treillage* of willow or painted chestnut, espalier fruit trees and bee-hives. Here in rustic splendour Jean Coeur-de-Roy was said to meditate; to read poetry and to savour the fragrance of rosemary crushed between his fingers.

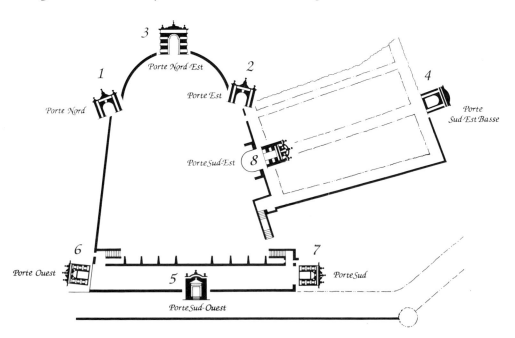

When we arrived Colonel Challan Belval, with sleeves rolled up and wearing a pair of old trousers and wellingtons, was mowing the grass. 'It's a lot of work – especially as we aren't here always, we're in Paris.' A tall, straight-backed elderly man, looking too young to be a great-grandfather, Challan Belval does all the work himself except for occasional help from his children. 'I've just mown it for your visit,' he said as he introduced his charming wife to us.

The present house goes back to the seventeenth century, the colonel and his wife explained as they pointed out the stables, the workshops used in the past for estate maintenance and a huge bread oven which had supplied the house with its daily bread. Not far from the buildings was a fine mulberry tree with a spreading head and heart-shaped leaves. 'There, you see that mulberry tree? In the nineteenth century they cultivated silkworms here – like in the Midi. But then because it's quite cool here – they stopped.'

Everything strident, buoyant, assertive and trenchant is missing. Lying half obliterated by long grass are fallen columns. 'We would like to restore that little column there,' Madame said. '*Alors*, we haven't done it yet.' The Colonel sighed with the onerous fatigue of trying to keep the place with some semblance of shape and substance. 'There's such a lot of work to do.' He pointed out where there had once been terraces, where once there had been defence towers to match the remaining one. '*Alors*, when I was young I remember there was a tower standing here – the same as that one. I don't know what was on these terraces. I think there was vegetation, but I'm not sure because we don't have any papers. Nothing. Perhaps in Dijon one might find something.' The weariness of his burden seemed to permeate the very heart of the garden. He and his wife were fighting for breath; breath for their estate and for the garden – while scarlet poppies made inroads amongst the dishevelled roses.

'This is "Reine d'Hollande",' the colonel said showing us some scrambling roses still in bud against the walls. 'That one is very, very old – I don't know – it's *blanc nacré*, pearly. That rose? That one – I can't remember very well. I should know because it was I who put it in.' Then looking at an espalier with a thick trunk and noduled branches he said, 'Usually it has masses of fruit, but this year it got burnt by the frost. *Alors*, normally we can eat fruit up to the month of March.'

Although the colonel spoke quietly, without demonstrative passion, there was an undertow of ardour as he talked of the trees planted by his grandfather about a hundred years ago. One was a magnolia which had just finished flowering, another was a ginkgo. 'We call it *l'arbre aux écus* because in autumn the leaves look like gold coins.' Like the antediluvian

Gate one on the plan, leading into parched fields up the Auxois.

Wellingtonia on the Beauregard estate, ginkgos too go back a long way. They are the only trees living today that have survived unchanged for about a hundred and sixty million years – give or take a digit or two. He pointed to a magnificent tree growing in the field just beyond one of the most imposing gates. '*Alors là*, there's an oak tree. It's perhaps three hundred years old but it has been struck by lightning two or three times, and in the hurricane . . . well, a branch fell down, it struck the arch – but this *porte* did not move. We were lucky. Only some of the *couronnement* has been repaired a little. The *boule* on the left. *Vous voyez?* That is new, and also over there where the stones are whiter than others.' And people to do the restoration? 'Happily it is not hard to find people locally who work in stone.'

The acoustics within the walls are so remarkable that when a cousin of the colonel's played the flute standing on the tribune, the notes could be heard in all quarters of the garden. It was easy to imagine music floating and echoing round the enclosed arenas while guests strolled, half-tranced on wine and sensuality at twilight. No wonder the colonel and his wife felt the fabric of nostalgia running through their fingers.

Leading us to the grotto he showed us where there were once fountains and tanks; where the *'passage de canalisation'* had been constructed and how water had been collected from all the roofs of the village by an intricate system of waterways. 'Yet so much has disappeared . . .'. The sentence faded away. Then he added, rather wistfully, as though trying to make us comprehend how beautiful the garden once had been, 'The best time to see the garden is in the evening. In the month of July or August. Because in July the grass is mown, it's all cleared, the roses are out and the *portes* look good. Yes, July is the month, the beginning of July for the roses. And in the evening between five and six.' Then he added softly, almost to himself, remembering summers threading back to his childhood, 'It's so pretty – when the sun is going down.'

Not until we neared the house did the colonel perk up a bit as he showed us his nursery-bed full of young dahlias ready for planting out. Dahlias? In this setting of Renaissance nobility – where could they possibly be bearable? But a French gardener and his dahlias are inseparable. I ought to know by now, and who am I to wince, coming from a country with the outrageous habit of using feral heathers in their millions to disfigure flower-beds throughout Britain?

Madame Challan Belval called us in for tea. We sat in a drawing room of portraits, elegance and with a flavour as touching as the garden outside the long windows. Madame, pouring tea from a magnificent and ancient pewter teapot, was as gentle and courteous as her husband, and I felt we could have sat long in that drawing-room listening to their stories of the past history of the estate and of the colonel's years in the cavalry in Algeria, Morocco and Indo-China, and looking at photograph albums showing the garden flourishing in its prime of life. And when he admitted, what I had already felt was inevitable, that not one of his children would carry on after his death, I felt there was even more reason to linger.

Reluctantly we left, knowing that if ever we came back things would have slipped a little further. How fortuitous to have seen the garden now, so beautiful, faded and insubstantial. On our way to the car the colonel showed us the stables. 'Here was where we kept the *calèche*, here our hunting carriage, the *voiture de chasse*.' The place was shadowy, with still a slight taint of hay mixed with manure in the air. Solidly built with wooden stalls, iron mangers and cobbled floors, I half expected to hear the sharp, unmistakable click as a horse shifted its weight from one leg to another. 'My grandfather had horses,' the colonel said quietly as we turned back towards the sunlight, 'I still remember the last two that were here.'

THROUGH GALLERIES OF
GREEN TWILIGHT

This garden, private and enchanting, acts as a consolatory counter-balance to the previous two. Unlike the Marquise de Beauregard and Colonel Challan Belval, the owners here have perhaps found one solution to the threatening problem of how to maintain a castle and its estate. The marquis and his wife are young and energetic; for two years now they have persevered in their determination to make something commercially viable out of their inherited estate without destroying its ancient nobility. That part, the commercial bit, does not come into this account. What does, is the garden. And it is because of the ghostly finger-prints which still linger about its stately walls, topiary, pools and paths, that I felt the garden should follow on from Colonel Challan Belval's at Moutier Saint-Jean.

Stendhal and the Doubs are inextricably tangled in my thoughts ever since I read *Le Rouge et le Noir*, when I longed to find the setting of the novel. Looking down on the valley of the Doubs, Stendhal wrote: 'Over on its western slopes five or six more valleys wind back into the mountains, in each of which the eye picks out a number of little streams tumbling down from one cascade to another, to fall at last into the river. The sun strikes hot in these mountains, but even when its light is shining full upon them, here, on this terrace, magnificent plane trees protect the traveller and his dreams.'

This is indeed a country to dream about. With forests, gorges and lakes, with the meandering course of the river Doubs and its small, sequestered villages within touching distance of serious mountains, the lovely cathedral of Strasbourg and the Italian frontier, it is an area of France where I could easily take root. It is an area, too, permeated by strange legends of werewolves, imps and fairies. Tales which are still passed down from generation to generation.

And it was here in the region known as the Franche-Comté, having a morning to spare before our next garden rendez-vous, that Tamsin rang the owner of the Château de Bournel at Cubry. Could we possibly come to visit his garden the next morning as early as convenient? Without having written beforehand, such intrusiveness on a Sunday morning might have received a dusty answer. We were prepared. But instead, the owner, the Marquis de Moustier, seemed to think it the most natural request, only explaining that he was involved in a golf tournament on his land and that later in the morning we would have to excuse him.

For five hundred years the property has been in the family. In 1496 Jean de Moustier and his wife settled into a fortified castle, south of the present one, in the tiny hamlet of Nans which on a fine day can be seen from the terrace of the château. It was not until about 1735 that Louise de Bournel, wife of the first marquis, decided to build the château here on its present site at Cubry.

Two years ago the marquis and the marquise opened part of their château as a hotel with fifteen bedrooms, lounges, a bar and restaurant. In eighty hectares of 'English' parkland they have made an eighteen-hole golf course among century-old trees, water courses and undulating landscape. It is too soon yet to know how it will work out. 'But it's good that the region of the Franche Comté have been helping us for a year now,' the marquis told us. 'It's not very much – but it helps!'

The garden to the château is private. 'It is very old. And it has been the same since the eighteenth century. It is also very French,' the marquis explained, as he walked with us towards the garden under the château with its long windows, pepper-pot turrets and steep roofs decorated with a chevron enrichment of gold and terracotta tiles. To the right of us was a line of golfers. Their bright outfits made them look like a row of decorative tulips in a London park. In the morning sunlight each stood on his allotted patch practising hitting balls towards the distant horizon.

The immediate impression on walking into the garden was one of amazement. Unbelievably tall espaliered fruit trees were so huge and gnarled, their girth like elephant legs and their sinewy black arms showing the scars of many generations of pruning, that they formed vast architectural arches. Never have I seen such tunnels. Never such vaulted dimensions, where some of the trees with as many as twelve outstretched limbs on either side, reached overhead to form cavernous galleries.

Walking through this green twilight the marquis told us how they were trying to conserve some of the trees while also replacing others. 'The trees are both apples and pears, but they are beginning to degenerate, so we want to find again the old, old race of fruits.' Without a trace of complaint but with factual detachment, he remarked: 'We must do a lot of work.'

Overlooking the garden on one side are cedars planted on rising land so that they form a black background almost blocking out the sky. Dominating the overall design of the garden are three circular *bassins* fed by

She will sigh for you at the drop of a pebble.

rain collected from the rooftops: a system that has lasted through countless generations. 'The *bassins* have remained the same for more than two hundred years,' said the marquis. 'We have some watercolours which show the three levels just as they are.' Surrounding the large stone pools are four slightly curved oval vessels made of unadorned iron, adding static emphasis to the four quarters of the pools. These, at different levels in the centre of the garden, rise to the third *bassin*, built with baroque splendour out of the upper terrace which forms a concave background to the pool and to two stone figures.

'*C'est l'homme qui ouvre le rocher, et sort une source. L'eau – c'est la femme!*' In crepuscular gloom the figure of a man, looking for the water source, leans over the woman, who lies supine, symbolizing water springing from the rock. Beneath them the murky stillness of the dark water reflects their figures with pristine clarity. 'Look!' The marquis said. 'There is also something very nice.' He bent down, picked up a tiny pebble and threw it into the pool. '*Dans un moment après ça, on a l'impression qu'elle respire!*' In a moment the ripples had reached the reflection of the woman whose bosom rose and fell in a series of impassioned sighs.

A double flight of steps on either side of the pool and flanked at the top by a pair of mythical creatures with long toenails and curly-haired briskets, takes you to an ornate gate leading into part of the park. Here are cherries and magnolias, a fine collection of woodland trees, and an avenue of limes. On either side of the gate, running the whole length of the terrace, tall hedges have windows cut at regular intervals out of the box. Turn back. Look across the falling geometry of the garden; across the square given over to lawn; to another planned for flowers; and lower down across the *potager* to where, beyond, more parkland becomes one with the blueness of the horizon. The kitchen garden, prescriptive, restrained and comely, has always been there. Now it daily provides produce for the restaurant: fresh vegetables, soft fruit such as strawberries, raspberries and currants. And there are, too, families of peaches and mirabelle plums, as well as the collection of newly planted apples, pears and cherries.

Against the château, where hand-wrought iron staves are fixed at regular intervals, there had once been vines and fruit trees reaching almost up to the eaves. Here a dilapidated greenhouse, pretty and elegant, butts up to the château wall. It has a narrow flight of iron steps up one side, leading to a miniature gallery running the length of the glass-paned roof – the access for cleaning and repairs. Though no longer in use, its decorative utility is an example of the charm of rusting iron amongst flowers and foliage. Nearby, the cold frames still have some small old panes of hand-made glass.

'Here you see, *c'est une gloriette, une tonnelle.* The left part is all down, so we must repair it.' And the marquis led us up a double flight of mossy steps to a kind of elongated arbour made from great iron hoops, and an elaborately scrolled iron bench. It was charming and light-hearted, as though some master craftsman had done a little spontaneous doodling in metal.

The marquise, whose children are two, six and eight, came into the garden to gather some herbs. Her enthusiasm for restoring the garden was heartfelt. Her plan was to mix vegetables and flowers as a *mélange* of practicality and luxuriance. 'I have already planted one hundred old roses, but there are lots more to plant.' Roses are arranged in descending grades of colour, beginning with deep black-red ones on the upper level, through mauves and pinks to white ones at the lower end of the garden where there are swathes of blue irises and crimson peonies.

A gentle warfare is waged over what she and her husband want to do in the garden, and what the eldest of the three gardeners, who has been there thirty years, thinks is appropriate. She remarked somewhat sardonically, 'I fear he might plant onions in the middle of the paths!'

The garden is full of promise. If Louise de Bournel occasionally haunts the garden where everything remains walled, proportioned and graceful, she must find solace now to discover the present owners restoring her original inspiration with painstaking dedication. Wherever snow or disease has turned the dark green of the box hedges outlining so much of the garden into discoloured patches, look carefully, and you will see a new plant already in place. Behind the precision of the box, roses are neatly tied along horizontal wires, while others, such as the wildly lavish 'Rambling Rector' and 'Blush Rambler', entwined with clematis 'Ernest Markham', 'Snow Queen' and 'Little Nell', form overhead shade.

If Stendhal found the Doubs a dream, this garden has the same quality. It may not be identical to the original form, but there is new impetus at work among the bay trees, the fruit and the clematis. And there is an encouraging sense of revival alongside the old decorative ironwork which has for generations stabilized the pliancy of flowers and the languor of roses.

CEREBRAL GARDENERS

QUINCIZE – AN EIGHTEENTH-CENTURY GARDEN

'What makes the difference between Britain and France is that we have Napoléon and Brigitte Bardot.' This laconic statement was made to us by the Vicomte de Bourgoing as we stood surveying the princely layout of his eighteenth-century garden in the Morvan. I suppose we looked non-plussed. It was ten in the morning; Cassandra was being entertained by Marguerite, the young daughter of the vicomte, and we were sheltering under umbrellas in a state of anticipation for a garden which had been highly recommended by Louis Benech.

The Morvan, in Burgundy, is a regional '*parc*' full of flowing streams and forests of beech and oak, where no hill exceeds 3,000 feet and where an occasional western wind – the *vent de la pluie* – sweeps through the sparse and peaceful pastures enclosed by hedges. I have never been there when it is not raining.

Quincize is a magnificent estate reached by a long avenue of ash trees planted at the turn of the century. And like so many others in France it has been affected by Napoléon Bonaparte. 'The whole legal system in France goes back to him!' said the vicomte. 'And so it has remained – for about two hundred years. Because of the *code Napoléon*, huge estates don't exist in France as they do in the UK. They and their contents have been divided up. When a man has four children, all of them must inherit equally.' The system has sliced up estates for generations. 'And now,' the vicomte concluded, 'Brigitte Bardot has added her influence to Napoléon's! Houses in the old days were meant to be built east and west. East was the entrance, west was the garden. But Bardot invented sun-tan – so now houses have to face south!'

The present owners live in Paris but come frequently to the Morvan and are restoring the gardens according to old maps which show the original layout as well as subsequent alterations made by succeeding generations, adding to and amending what their ancestors had first designed. From the moment she set eyes on the place, Catherine de Bourgoing felt inspired to breathe life into the garden again. She is sensitive to its history but feels unconstrained by its past.

PREVIOUS PAGE
From across the upper terrace at Quincize to the distant Morvin countryside.

In the library, leather-bound books in many languages covering the walls from floor to ceiling, are the maps. 'My uncle of a long time ago collected books. His wife collected silver. As they had no children, my side of the family got the books, and the other side of the family got the silver.' Then the vicomte added with a slightly droll expression: 'My uncle died in 1870 – and we haven't purchased a book since then!'

The first of the finely drawn and painted maps was made in the seventeenth century. It shows in detail how in 1630 the château had been built on the traditional design of the *corps de logis* (the residential part), the forecourt, offices, farm buildings and four towers surrounding a central courtyard with a well in the centre. Set amongst arable land with just a few oxen and cows, it was enclosed by walls against robbers as the countryside was insecure during *la Fronde*, the uprisings during the early years of Louis XIV's reign. The *seigneur* of Quincize had the right to deliver '*haute, basse et moyenne justice*' in the name of the king. In 1780 quite radical alterations were made: two of the towers came down, an orangery was constructed under the terrace (not unlike, though on a far more modest scale, the majestic orangery at Meudon, south-west of Paris); and the parterre, the ornamental flower garden in the courtyard, was reconstructed behind the house in the design of *un fer à cheval*, a horseshoe, outlined in box.

The second map has an *Explication des chiffres* – an index explaining the numbered sections. 'Number one,' Jean-Marie de Bourgoing pointed out, 'is called château and *cour d'honneur*' (the main courtyard). 'Two is the *cour d'entrée*; three is the *parterre*, so flowers were there.' The *parterre* had probably been divided into those parts which were for cutting flowers such as pinks, pansies, stocks and columbines, while in another section there would have been plants for scent, which might have included hyssop, basil, wormwood, clary and rosemary. 'Four is the *potager*, divided into eight sections.' Traditionally the sections were arranged in strips of varying width according to the vegetables grown. 'Five is *boulingrin*. You should know about it because it is English! It's an old expression which doesn't exist any more. It comes from 'bowling green', which at the time was fashionable in France.' Often the *boulingrin* was just a sunken lawn or a turf *parterre*. 'Number six is the *ancien verger*,' he said, pointing to it on the map 'And then, so on and so on . . . there was a *bosquet* and a park there.' (A *bosquet*, an ornamental 'green room', a shrubbery or thicket, varied in elaboration from those with fountains as at Versailles to groves divided by simple grassy walks as at Quincize.)

Everything was shown on the map: the broad paths dividing the *potager* from the garden; the gate leading to the orchard; the trellis which might have supported roses and jasmine; espaliers, hedges and walls and the orangery. 'The orange trees died in the 'twenties as they had to have heat every winter, but my brother, who lives a few kilometres from here, has got orange trees which go back to the eighteenth century. Now they too are starting to die, but he is replacing them.'

Outside, we walked down the steps from the terrace where in summer the *parterre* will be filled with a flamboyant effect of dark red roses and orange dwarf dahlias, to where their one gardener was working in the kitchen garden. On either side of the steps are brilliant roses, 'Joseph's Coat', and beneath the terrace are two vast cisterns for collecting rain water from the roofs, some oleanders which have to be housed inside the orangery each winter, and an old vine which the vicomte admitted was useless. Along here Catherine de Bourgoing has started filling triangles, made from zig-zag box hedging, with herbs. She is also restoring the box which outlines the vegetables, by assiduously taking cuttings every August. 'I still have another 180 metres to fill!'

Bordering the paths are espalier fruit trees. 'They are old. The wife of my distant uncle who collected books, loved gardens. It was she who planted them so they are more than a hundred years old.' And because Catherine de Bourgoing passionately wanted to perpetuate the tradition of espaliered fruit trees, she took a course on pruning and grafting at the Luxembourg Gardens in Paris. At the same time she started to read. Everything inspirational or practical on gardening was devoured, including all the books of Gertrude Jekyll and Vita Sackville-West. Her first clematises, brought back from Wisley four years ago, have now prolifer-ated into a Sissinghurst tangle of clematis and roses clambering up fruit trees. And after a visit to the rose garden at Bagatelle in the Bois de Boulogne, she came away inspired to grow bushes as voluptuous and extravagant as those great two-metre high creatures she had seen there. *Rosa moschata*, 'Blanche Moreau', 'Blanc de Vibert' and 'The Nun' are among a border of white roses; the red shrubs include 'Gloire de Ducher' and the small but spectacular, 'Charles de Mills'. 'Claire Jacquier', that most equable of eggy-coloured climbers, adorns one corner of a vegetable square while trios of the freely branching 'Clair Matin' decorate others. Catherine de Bourgoing says: 'I choose the roses which have the best decorative effect and which flower twice.' In between the roses she plants hardy perennials.

'I love the peonies planted a hundred years ago by the aunt who collected silver,' she said. 'I give them a lot of manure and take great care because she had lovely species. I am starting a collection of peonies.' She is also

The precision of a potager is easy to maintain compared to the painstaking restoration of the flower garden.

collecting hydrangeas and hellebores – those sombre flowers of exquisite fragility which appear just when you despair of winter ever loosening its hold on spring. In spite of the dampness of the Morvan and late frosts, lavender does well. A huge circular bed of it, cropped to perfection, stands in the centre of the *potager*, surrounded by four balls of yew. As Jean-Marie de Bourgoing said, looking at the serene composure of this design without a scrap of recklessness about it: 'Well! It is the French spirit! We don't let go.' Then he added: 'We aren't good with nature!'

'Come, I'll show you the *bosquet* which has remained the same shape for almost two hundred years.' But as we walked towards it, everything we had seen – the *parterre*, the terraces, the orangery and the kitchen garden – fell from our sight as our eyes were drawn on that grey, gentle day in spring to the avenue of limes leading away from the garden towards the park. These limes are huge and theatrical. They have been so ruthlessly amputated for years, in a way for which only the French have such a brilliant and inherent flair, that by now their crowns are writhing contortions of mutilated branches. Chinese bound feet have nothing on this deliberate bondage. The whole distorted effect was softened by a thick fleece of grey moss so that as we walked beneath the trees in that vaporous moisture, we were like swimmers moving between great stalagmites of underwater coral. It was enchantment and it was beautiful. The pollarding, which is all done by hand, takes place every other year. How lucky we were to see it on such a melancholy day, for soon all the little sprouts of fresh growth would appear, and by midsummer the avenue would be a mass of shapely green and the aquatic, underwater landscape would have evaporated. In the meantime, thank goodness for the 'French spirit' that can never 'let go'.

After taking us through a *bosquet* of a few newly planted rhododendrons ('It would not have been done in the eighteenth century, but we couldn't resist our acid soil!') beneath tall trees with long grass full of violets underfoot and paths between high hornbeam hedges which once had formed a labyrinth, the vicomte led us to the pool.

A few hundred yards below the gardens the pool lay calm and serene, an unembellished eye in the centre of a flat piece of land where the views of the Morvan stretched for twenty miles. It was *une pièce d'eau* built from stone at the end of the eighteenth century, in a shape which the vicomte admitted had no significance that he knew of, in spite of its intriguing design. It is a design found in Persian carpets where the stylized garden pattern represents a central platform surrounded by water under a floral canopy. The shape is contrived from a square imposed on four small circles as though to represent both controlled formality and the abstract serenity of paradise. The identical shape exists in the gardens of the Alhambra and in the Mughal gardens of India.

It was this pool and the tortured lime trees which were to remain our strongest memories of the ancient domain of Quincize. As we left, the vicomte urged us to come back again when the weather was better and the roses were in flower. But there was just one more thought: his children. Would they one day take over the maintenance of Quincize? 'Ah,' he said with an expressive shrug: 'That is the question we ask every generation.'

LE JARDIN DES CINQ SENS

From the air the garden looks like an intriguing structure of minute intricacy. Fastidious paths slice through espaliers, and geometric plantings form diamond-shaped lattices. Not until you see the figure of a tiny human being beside one of the surrounding garden walls do you get a sense of proportion. The garden is not an embroidered sampler. It is a place to walk through; a place to test your responses.

Yvoire is a medieval village of four hundred inhabitants built on a promontory which separates the 'Petit Lac' of Léman from the 'Grand Lac'. Arriving by water on some morning when the lake is calm and silky, and the sun has not yet dispersed a low mist that hides the surrounding hills, all you see are tumbling waves of foliage and the château. The garden is hidden. We soon found out why. The Marquise de Beauregard's acerbic comment on the village of Yvoire was understandable: 'Ghastly! Ghastly!'

The day we went, a Sunday in May, a slow river of tourists was flowing like treacle to and fro through the narrow lanes of cafés, ice-cream bowers and '*artisan*' shops full of junk, on their way to the lakeside port or back again to where cars stretched endlessly on the outskirts of the village. But step aside. Walk through the gateway into the Garden of the Five Senses, which lies at the back of the steep-roofed château, and you enter an undisturbed world where you can make an Epicurean meander. Although the garden is in the heart of the village and open to the public, there was barely a soul about. All was quiet, all was peaceful, and you felt you might be entering the cloistered garden of some secluded monastery.

The château, which in fact is the keep of a fifteenth-century fortress, has been inhabited by the family of the present occupants, Yves and Anne-Monique d'Yvoire, since 1655. The garden covers only a quarter of a hectare and is surrounded by the high walls of the original castle kitchen garden. The decline of the *potager* was slow. Gradually the Yvoire family neglected it, until it was left to the priest and a few old ladies of the village to carry on the cultivation. When they too relinquished their commitment the *potager* reverted to wilderness.

For a long time the young d'Yvoires had wanted to create something

Still in its infancy, the 'woven' garden will one day form a pattern of white roses and silvery wild oats.

that was not just another castle garden for visitors, of the kind that can be found anywhere. The government offered no help and the garden would have to pay for itself, so it needed infinite patience as well as ruthless decision to sift through ideas and find the answer. The place is a classified site yet there had been suggestions that a commercial fairground would be the solution! But, as Anne-Monique d'Yvoire said, 'We wanted something beautiful which would relate to the history of the place and not just a leisure park.' After chasing numerous ideas with the professional advice of a landscape architect, Alain Richert, and a landscape constructor, André Gayraud, they decided on *Le Labyrinthe aux Oiseaux*.

The landscapers were intrigued by the idea of a labyrinth, but at the same time they wanted to resurrect the *potager* with its paths, pool and fruit trees, its culinary and medicinal plants, based on a design of the Middle Ages. The garden should be both imaginative and symbolic; both of botanical interest and for pleasure. It took a year of drafting and re-drafting, of discussion and fine tuning before they agreed on the final design. In September 1986 the work began. The land needed clearing and terracing; there had to be drainage channels and automatic drop-by-drop irrigation. Flower borders were edged with wooden boards, and the pool and aviary were constructed. In the spring of 1988 the garden was finally opened to the public.

It is divided into distinct enclosures on two levels. In describing it you have to keep in mind how diminutive it is. There are no impressive perspectives, no spacious terraces or regal proportions and no compelling grandeur to stun you with overwhelming awe. Passion and unrestraint are alien to the place. Instead the garden is intimate and exquisite, offering a mixture of intellectual and sensual impact while maintaining an air of great poise and decorum.

On the upper level, near the entrance, is an 'alpine meadow' built around a stone which was so immovable that Madame d'Yvoire thought of it as a *'clin d'oeil à la montagne'* – a glimpse of a mountain – which inspired the choice of violets, fritillaries and alpine tulips, jonquils, saxifrages, gentians, and many other upland plants interspersed among stones and decorative grasses and chosen to flower at different times.

Beyond the alpine rectangle is a geometric latticework, *un tissage*, or woven garden, which springs instantly into focus from bone-white Rugosas. These fragrant roses, 'Blanc Double de Coubert', are interwoven with unsophisticated *avoine bleue rustique*, silvery-blue wild oats cut into *'boules'*, looking like lavender and low enough to allow views onto the lower garden. Madame d'Yvoire loves the effect these two plants make.

She describes the rose as marvellously perfumed and *raffiné*, while the garden designer thought of the 'weaving' of white roses and wild grasses as a symbol of the garden – '*une herbe folle et, au contraire, un rosier très raffiné.*'

Here, on the upper side of the garden, deliberately sited to hide ugly neighbouring walls, is the 'undergrowth' garden. Seven lime trees, *Tilia* x *moltkei* with slightly pendulous branches, are underplanted with woodruff, soft ferns, *Polystichum setiferum*, and *Brunnera macrophylla* looking like upmarket forget-me-nots.

On the other side of the *tissage* is a green cloister; a place for meditation and repose where columns of hornbeam join one to another to form arches and the walls are covered in honeysuckles. The '*cloître de verdure*', as it is named, is divided by low box hedges into four small gardens. Based on a monastery design two hundred years old, medicinal and aromatic plants were prudently cultivated by the monks for their pungent, piercing or bitter scent to counteract the stench of sewage which in summer hung about the cloisters. For the lean days when there was little to eat, the wily monks planted honeysuckles for the blackbirds, knowing their partiality for the shelter of its foliage and for the berries in winter. They were easily trapped. Here, contained within the four beds, are rue, santolina, thyme, rosemary, peppermint, camomile, balm, salvia, savory, wild thyme and hyssop – much beloved by bees – growing around a central granite bird-pool trickling water. Madame d'Yvoire said about this garden: '*J'avoue avoir un faible pour la rue*' – a weakness for rue because for her it has the scent of warm figs. But scent varies from person to person, as Madame Simonet in the Drôme so persuasively told us. For some, rue can be ambrosial, smelling of perfumed oils, honey and oranges, while others recoil with repugnance, complaining of tom cats marking their territory.

Descend from the cloister garden down a few steps to the labyrinth, laid out exactly to the design of an ancient *potager*. This is the Garden of the Five Senses. Four gardens are surrounded by paths made of gravel from the mountains, flanked by fan-shaped fruit trees and hedging of common hornbeam, *Carpinus betulus*. But the hedging is decorated with strands of sweet peas which use the hornbeam as supports, so that all those washed colours of blue, pink, mauve and crimson intertwine among the shiny leaves of the hedge.

The first garden here is the '*jardin du goût*', with a variety of tastes: it has strawberries, raspberries, blackcurrants, blueberries; rhubarb, onions, lovage and celery; an orange tree with edible flowers, and apple trees, some of which produce fruit weighing half a kilo each.

The second is the garden of scents, the '*jardin de l'odorat ou des parfums*', which includes alliums, honeysuckles, viburnums, the nettle-shaped lemon balm smelling of soap and good for keeping mosquitoes away with its piercingly citrous smell; tobacco plants, mahonias, a medlar which produces squashy brown fruit, and daphnes smelling faintly of cloves. And roses. One of these, a moss rose, 'Blanche Moreau', has an unfortunate tendency to chronic mildew, but in a good season has lush white flowers smelling of fruit infused in camomile.

I must stop here for a moment to say a word about the family of moss roses. Among them are some of the most beautiful of all roses; not just for their flowing names, such as *Rosa* x *centifolia* 'Muscosa', or even for their whiskers, but because when the mossy buds and the crumpled petals are seen together the combination of colour and texture is hard to beat. How lucky that some rogue mutation took place generations ago so that in our gardens we can fall in love with 'William Lobb'. His heavy-headed flowers are deep magenta mixed with dark grey. His green-mossed buds grow in clusters – involuntarily you put out your hand to touch.

The garden of touch, the *'jardin des textures'*, is full of fine- or coarse-leafed plants in tones of silver, grey and gold: euphorbia, mahonia, inula, bronze fennel and wormwood. And there is meadow-rue, *Thalictrum aquilegifolium*, with an airy appearance from the grey-green leaves and pink fluffy flowers which blur the asphodels, hellebores, irises, lady's mantle and *Aruncus sylvester* – known as goat's beard or, in France, *Barbe du Loup*.

In the *'jardin des couleurs'* are variations of blue: campanulas, primulas, iris sibiricas, violets, gentians and quite the best azure geranium, 'Johnson's Blue'. And there are meconopsis, those paragons of poppies whose range of blue varies from cobalt to cerulean and aquamarine; whose petals are flimsy though their colour is of amaranthine density whether you see them singly, as vivid as a roller bird tumbling in the air, or in a mass like a piece of misplaced sky.

The sense of hearing is symbolized by the large aviary in the centre of the four gardens, built over a fountain and an ancient tank. Here are ducks, pheasants and pairs of turtle doves. In another smaller aviary, overgrown with a scented climber, *Araujia sericofera* (which Madame d'Yvoire refers to by its synonym, *Physianthus albus*), are doves, quails and other small birds. The water from the fountain and the soothing coo of turtle doves makes a continuous backcloth of sound, against which the garrulous chatter of sparrows and the indeterminate song of other birds are superimposed.

Somewhere in the garden, but I can no longer remember where, there were small rumpled roses, 'Cardinal de Richelieu', with mauvy-pink buds opening to rich, almost purple flowers which become dirtier as they age till

In among the hornbeam arches are places to sit in the garden of repose.

they look like contusions. And I noticed somewhere else a clematis, that stagy *Clematis montana* 'Grandiflora' which has unscented white flowers eight centimetres across.

Though the garden is young there are a few mature plants still growing as a legacy from the d'Yvoire ancestors – a vine along one wall, old fruit trees (some a hundred years old) and a half-dead cherry tree supporting *Rosa filipes* 'Kiftsgate', that climbing rose with massive festoons of creamy white flowers with bright yellow stamens. There are two rare trees, favourites of Madame d'Yvoire, planted long ago by the great-grandfather of her husband. One is a persimmon which produces magnificent fruit at the end of the season, the other a tender *Lagerstroemia indica* with smooth, strangely mottled grey and cinnamon bark and flowers of crinkled lilac-pink petals. The tree needs warmth, so the Savoie is an alien province to find it growing in, but by late September she calls it the '*roi du jardin*'.

Anne-Monique d'Yvoire has a passion for bold plants, particularly for the angelica and acanthus growing in the garden. The former is dominating, growing sometimes to six feet, and if you burn the seeds and root it fills your house with fragrance; the latter has stately spikes and incised leaves of great distinction. She loves too a species lilac, *Syringa microphylla*, small, with downy leaves and a cloyingly sweet scent; euphorbias for their acid yellow flowers in spring; perennial geraniums for their blue, and sages for their tough purple leaves. *Gaura lindheimeri*, a most graceful and slender perennial from Texas, is another plant she looks forward to, when its white and rosy-pink flowers appear 'like the wings of butterflies'.

If you visit the garden come with an open mind. For though it is almost a year since we visited Yvoire, the garden is still adolescent. At the foot of the cherry tree the 'Kiftsgate' rose had not yet become headstrong; its wilful tendency to take over a tree was still malleable. Against the walls the clematis were at the immature stage when each tendril was under control, pinned like a delicate tracery of potential summer. Too many garden bones were visible where plants had not yet taken up their allotted space. And the hornbeam hedges, being young and spiky, left the garden transparent. In time the paths will be narrow, confining and architectural; they will compel you to walk from one enclosure to another, testing your senses and evoking an almost spiritual tranquillity. Anne-Monique d'Yvoire says: 'The garden is still young – and there remains so much to do before it becomes anything like our dreams.'

STONE, LAVENDER AND A
LOVE OF SPHERES

'When you say you like a garden without flowers – they kill you! People say, "Where *is* your garden?" They kill me, kill me!' These dramatic words were spoken by a finely-boned lady of seventy-four standing in her garden of colours so distilled that each one had been tapped for its fundamental essence.

This was a garden unlike anything else I had seen in France, and the spareness of its quality made me feel like a rumpled intruder. Madame de Vésian herself was dressed in fine cotton the colour of the underside of mushrooms and her white hair, drawn back tightly, was as smooth as the stones in her garden.

Travelling towards the Lubéron on the deserted autoroute south of Orléans, where on the bridge-embankments tiny plants surrounded by black circles of plastic looked like an orderly skin disease and in the fields cows lay in the shade like spilt clotted cream, we gulped up acres of agricultural France. The beautifully engineered road, with Rugosa roses flowing down the centre in a stream of pink, crimson and white good enough to suck, swooped on down to Clermont-Ferrand. Sunday in Brioude, and everyone was trimming a Virginia creeper or tending allotments, while north of Le Puy wild narcissus lay in scented swathes among the hills. We passed fields of lavender not yet in flower before reaching the savage country of the Ardèche, powerful and magnificent in a thunderstorm with mountainsides of chestnuts, holm oak and wild cherries. Down towards Avignon were tidily cultivated fields and vineyards, and around Venasque, where signs were in Spanish, not German or English, the itinerant Spanish cherry-pickers sometimes stayed the whole summer, living with the farm workers until the *vendanges*. The young cherry trees were planted in rows between belts of wheat, giving an effect so textural it was hard from a distance to make out if they were trees or lavender bushes. Lavender here was used in motorway roundabouts instead of salvias, and whenever we stepped from the car we heard overhead the high trilling of invisible larks.

We had come to see a garden on the slopes of the Montagne du Lubéron, with its Romanesque churches and old villages of Ménerbes, Lacoste and Bonnieux, a garden which in its asceticism was the mirror-image of its owner. We had no intimation beforehand that we would find a garden where austerity and design could combine so brilliantly with the paramount practicalities of making and maintaining it.

Entering Nicole de Vésian's house we crossed her hall, walking over loose, smooth pebbles. Where most people have carpets or tiles or something static, we had the impression of a moving shoreline under our feet. We did not know then that this was an eloquent language which was carried on, faultless and immaculate, throughout the house and into her garden: a love of smooth surfaces, of circles, arcs and curves, of clean spheres and unembellished outlines is at the very heart of Madame de Vésian's world. 'I have a passion for stones. You know, I bought this place because first I wanted to buy the stones. The more stones poured out, the more I wanted it.'

Nicole had prepared a lunch for us as exquisite and unadorned as everything she had created both in and out of the house. On a terrace of pebbles and slabs of stone paving we sat on folding chairs the colour of leaves of lavender at a table covered with a coarse white linen cloth. The plants in the foreground reflected the curves of the distant landscape. The crusty bread, the large bowl of black olives, the tomatoes, salad and green olive oil and the cool rosé were all of the region; there were new potatoes and an omelette stuffed with herbs and sprinkled with basil; goat's cheese and dishes of strawberries and cherries followed – the only sign of red to be seen anywhere in the garden.

Born and brought up in Paris though her father was Welsh, Nicole worked for years in the fashion house of Hermès. Three years ago she started to make her garden in the Lubéron, in a village that once had 3,500 people in it but which now has 800. 'They don't very much like foreigners, but they begin to accept them now.' Cherries and vines are being replanted and when a farmer can sell his house with six hectares of land, he builds himself 'an awful modern house with plastic and he is happy'. In her own house there used to be four or five families living. 'My friends thought me mad. The house was a catastrophe. It was so difficult, so ugly. There was such a wild landscape with trees falling apart and no view – I saw nothing but junk.' Then as if to prove her sanity by stressing each word she said, 'But underneath were stones.'

This fact would have sent any other gardener running to a part of France where the soil was deep and fertile, but not Nicole. She is a stone addict; if her soul were visible it would be nothing like '*l'Âme entre son Ange Gardien*

The terrace where not a flower is permitted to show its face.

et le Demon' on a capital at Saint-Benoit-sur-Loire, where the Soul looks so pathetic and submissive between its Guardian Angel and the Demon; it would be a beautiful stone as emphatic as all the others in her garden.

Wherever you look walls, ledges, alcoves and edgings have been constructed in stone. Balls, sinks and troughs; segments of broken columns, seats and urns; all are complemented by the plants, each one of which is cut into a precise and immaculate '*boule*'. With her sure eye for weight, alignment and correlation her addiction to stone is never over-indulged.

'I am so attached to textures – very few people *feel* gardens, they just think about plants, about showing off, but I like to have only three plants. It's funny, you know, but I don't have many more. I am playing with rosemary, lavender, santolina and a little sage.' She says she is lazy, that she spurns sophisticated plants and looks for ones that are easy so that she does not have to worry about fresh soil and cultivation. What she does tackle with spirited enthusiasm are experiments with new shapes: a rose cut into the form of a tree, or her lavender and rosemary, which 'I bob and keep very slender so no one knows what kind of plants they are, or I let them half grow and cut them so often they become hairy, while with others I leave them alone to grow into free plants. So each treatment makes a difference.' She does the same with her thyme, keeping it either tightly cropped or allowing some to flower. By this method she produces two distinct effects with the same plant.

Two years ago, to achieve privacy from the road, she planted honeysuckle until it became a green wall, then cut it back ruthlessly so one minute it was all long and the next it was severed to the roots. The treatment was so effective it grew back even more vigorously. 'I want to be hidden but I want to see out – so now I cut whenever I need.'

Because the land drops steeply below the house, the garden descends in four terraces linked by worn steps where once the village ponies nimbly negotiated their way to the valley below. On one level, within the natural curve of the rock, are two shallow tanks of water, remains of the village reservoir dating from the Middle Ages. To give movement to contrast with their symmetry, Nicole has planted two loosely shaped rosemary bushes and a quince tree.

Subdued greys and green, white lavender and santolina, grow on another terrace amid small balls of rosemary which she grew from clippings. 'They are my children! I keep them very, very close so that the wood never shows.' She shapes plants so that they duplicate the curve of the mountain beyond, but now having planted so many she is beginning to feel she has overdone it. 'Soon there is going to be a big burst! So I must clip, snip and cut.' But clipping, snipping and cutting is obviously just what Nicole enjoys. There is nothing tentative about her use of secateurs. And just because she does plant so densely, she has no problem with watering. Once she tried putting in plastic pipes but kept cutting the pipes by mistake so gave up. 'But I must say, even last year when everyone had water problems, I didn't because everything is planted so tight.'

Any plant that looks a bit sickly goes into her hospital, a secluded and sheltered bed, where they stay a few months and are nourished on the right diet. When they have recovered she replants them in a different place. 'You see this rosemary has just come to the hospital. I shall take care of it until it is better.' We looked at a far from robust, rather scrappy bit of wood which might have defeated most people, but not Nicole who poured confidence into the plant at her feet. 'I think they like the change of place!'

She then pointed to her lilac. 'I cut it to death – and what happened? It grew magnificent flowers with no leaves – it was like cherry flowers – it was amazing!' A handsome white oak, *Quercus alba*, which she hurriedly rescued from the bulldozer, is bursting with vitality in spite of having been planted in June. 'People said I was mad but I left it big until this year when I cut it right back and look – it's doing so well.'

On a terrace of silvery plants, the flowers of *Senecio bicolor* were cut off entirely. 'I don't want yellow in the garden!' But yellow is not the only colour that is banished; the violet-flowering sages had been decapitated so that there were no colours anywhere – only the muted tones of achromatic plants. She planted white irises but each time, to her despair, they came out violet. The roses bought as white turned out pink, so she hid them among santolina and if they become too intrusive – off go their heads. Certainly any roses there are keep a very low profile. Then, as though to justify her love for order, she said with a lovely rippling laugh, infectious and young: 'Winter is nicer because everything is tidy, very peaceful and organized.'

Looking around, it did not seem to me that anything was behaving obstreperously, although it was late May. Nothing strayed, nothing behaved wantonly. All the plants were lopped and sheared into controlled mounds rising in wave after wave. Nothing had been overlooked or done on impulse; nothing had happened fortuitously. With an intellect as deliberate and judicial as the blade of a scalpel she had eradicated stray leaves, annihilated disarray and by blending one tone into another had achieved serene harmony. But how? A man does come to help her with the heavy work, and now when he digs up an ailing plant he too says, '*à l'hôpital, à l'hôpital!*', but the rest of the work she does herself, including the fastidious trimming of plants which is undertaken the moment a shrub or tree shows a tendency to digress.

'Honestly! I think plants adore to be cut. And I do it any time!' I could almost hear Anglo-Saxon gasps, remembering the crucial timing and anguished indecisions about when to prune. 'This hibiscus got huge so I had to cut it down.' For Nicole a compulsion to pare is at the heart of all her gardening. At strategic points huge baskets are placed to contain the results of her constant trimming.

'Here is an arbutus, and over there a bonsai box – it was squeezed against the house, so I took it away very carefully.' For two years Nicole kept the plant in a basin of shallow water covered in winter by a shepherd's cape. 'Keeping it like a child', was the way she described her cherishing. When the bonsai was strong enough she planted it where the stones and shadows beneath are as integral as the shape. In the courtyard, where she wanted a vertical and bold effect, she planted two cypress trees so close together as to form one dark column.

'This is syringa. Oh the smell! I was amazed! I came down here last night, I hadn't been for a week, it was still covered in flowers.' And when the flowers do die it goes without saying that she will give them a bold beheading. However, with the jasmine against the wall, which was there when she came and which fills the house with scent on a June evening, she does show restraint. With reluctant self-control she will give the jasmine a moderate trim once or twice in the winter.

There are cherries, apricots, peaches and plums; a place where 'newly-born lavender' will be planted into squares with balls at the centre of each square; a massive group of box which were growing like trees when she first came. She cut the plants to the bone and they turned totally yellow. Everyone said 'You're crazy, and I said yes, everyone knows I'm crazy and the box know it also. But then it turned out not too bad. I am always after them, I want to get them this way,' she made a rhythmical gesture with her hands, 'undulating.'

Lower down her land, where it is still a wilderness, are fig trees and a forest of raspberries: 'These are all de-planted from the garden – and those collypocks, pollyhocks – what do you call them? I couldn't stand them any more, they get so untidy, so I put them all down here. In the end I got mad at them and cut them all down.' There are thistles with fretted leaves and heads which later become purple, a sweet-scented choisya, and in the winter the earth turns to blue from the density of wild irises with their delicate reflexed petals and tightly sheathed stems.

'I don't know anything about plants, to be honest.' If her garden with its

The result of Nicole de Vésian's 'madness' is a textural garden of shorn shrubs.

corners of subdued colours and temperate design is the result of knowing nothing about plants, then let's all pray for ignorance. But of course Nicole does know what she is doing; any visitor entering either her house or her garden is well aware of a percipient sensitivity behind every room or terrace.

At an important conference which she attended, 'for the creators of big gardens and architects from Europe', where there were lectures and presentations lasting three days and where people could meet and discuss, 'I was astonished that there were no modern concepts. I dare say my garden is a bit modern. I was looking for modernity – well, not for modernity but I was looking for easage – for easy care. I was looking for something clean, neat and very graphic. A new concept: to remain with the roots of the classic but at the same time to have a new way of looking at a garden and of taking care of it.' But she found nothing at this gathering; no response to her philosophy. Nor even any response from a National Trust speaker who admitted to the audience his distress at the sight of visitors in the garden. Why should he contrive to produce flowers of blues, mauves and pinks when the public all walk round in their emerald or orange and yellow shirts? 'So when I met him afterwards I said, "You know I have an idea for your garden. Provide your visitors with a cotton cloak for the dominant colour for that month, that week – pink, violet or blue." And he looked at me and stared, as if I was absolutely crazy. Quite, quite crazy.'

Nicole de Vésian may be innovative, a solitary voice in the gardening world, but she has got her message through to her ten grandchildren. They may normally wear violent green, red or yellow, but will remind their mothers before visiting their grandmama that they need to be in stony, stringy colours. And in case I had not remembered, in a quiet understatement she reminded me: 'You see – I do like things to be in harmony.'

POSTSCRIPT

The book has to end somewhere. But let me set it out in strong clear words that the reason for ending with Nicole de Vésian is not because I have run out of gardens; I have run out of space. France is full of gardens to unearth. Not only did we visit many more gardens than I have included, but I have a file of names, addresses and introductions which, for all I know, might lead to quirky, exemplary, outrageous or polychrome gardens as yet unseen. I don't know. Some might sing with mind-blowing resonance; others might be duds. But one thing I do know, having written this book, is that there are gardeners in France willing to put down their trowels, give up their time and *talk*. Imagination, gusto and tenderness are as constant and varied as flowers.

After 1992, when frontiers are supposedly non-existent, how dispiriting it will be if the British style of gardening spreads like a homogeneous rash as far as Spain and Italy. More than ever it is imperative that we should keep our own gardening heads – our identities. At present it seems that only in Northern France, where the climate is similar to ours, do we find gardens that, had we dropped from space, could be mistaken for English ones. Elsewhere everywhere is delightfully foreign.

There is one last kind of garden I want to mention: a place which is neither a flower nor a kitchen garden and yet, found in some neglected corner of France, it is the antithesis of everything I have been saying about the French predeliction for order.

I am talking about a way of arbitrary planting which has immediate charm; where peas, onions and forget-me-nots, growing in lackadaisical disarray, are divided by random grass and gravel paths, with a shadowy turbulence overhead from lilac, wisteria or apple trees. Somehow, in England you never come across this kind of planting. I do not know why not. Perhaps we are too good at gardening? A gardener in Britain would be mortified by such trifling. A gardener in Britain gardens; or else he is not a gardener. I am sure other visitors from England know what I mean. You can come across such a place by looking over a wall in the countryside of the Corrèze or when leaning out of a window in a small town such as

Sisteron. But when I have called it a garden to a French person, I am contradicted. Instead I am shown '*un vrai jardin*', a dull patch of grass dotted with shrubs and plastic furniture, and just as spick and span as their confectionery shops – but with none of the same incentive to walk in.

One difficulty I have had in describing gardens is vocabulary. We are stuck with this one word, 'garden', to describe the discreet garden of Maryvonne Sentuc, municipal gardens made from bedding plants, Anne Simonet's hill-top courtyard, Villandry, or the garden at the château Beauregard on the Lake of Geneva. The word is inadequate; totally unsubtle and unrevealing. What we need in our English language are a few nouns to use as alternatives to 'garden' so that the great span of these creative places can be adequately named. Not to be compared, but just to be classified.

Gardening in France is in a state of revolution. As one Frenchman remarked: 'Now that things appear so instantly through the media – this thing with gardens is quite amazing! Ten years ago, you know, you couldn't find an old rose in any place in France – and now you can find them in several nurseries.' If Old Roses are the litmus paper to show what is happening in France, then a visit to André Eve's rose stand at Courson is demonstrative proof that we are living in the midst of a horticultural upheaval.

Finally, French gardeners, regardless of the kind of place they have, possess an enviable quality: a kind of *tant pis* philosophy, a sense of acceptance in the face of failure. Gardeners are not generally known for their sense of humour and the French are no exception, but they do possess a coolness, a dashing *sang-froid*. 'Plants must either grow or give up,' is how one man described his laid-back attitude towards his garden. Another gardener spoke with intensity about her need to touch the earth as a form of communion with nature, at the same time showing an imperturbable philosophy towards disasters: 'If things are killed, I don't grieve! I plant something else in its place immediately.' And perhaps more than anyone, Paul on his island put it most succinctly when he said of his plants, '*Eh bah*, if they die they aren't in the right place – if they grow, one can go on.'

A few pines left standing after the hurricane which struck Madame Sentuc's garden on an island off the coast of Brittany.

GARDENS OPEN TO THE PUBLIC

Les Roses Anciennes

Monsieur André Eve, 28 Faubourg d'Orléans, 45302 Pithiviers. (Tel: 38.30.01.30) Open Mondays and Saturdays from the end of May to the beginning of July and in September.

Le Labyrinthe aux Oiseaux

Yvoire, Douvaine 74140. (Tel: 50.72.88.80) Open every day from May to the end of October from 10 am to 7 pm.

Association les Roses Anciennes de la Bonne Maison

Madame Odile Masquelier, 99 chemin de Fontanières, La Mulatière, Lyon 69350. (Tel: 78.42.42.82) Open on Mondays from March to September (except August) or by appointment in May and June.

Pépinières Planbessin

Colette Sainte-Beuve, Castillon 14490. (Tel: 31.92.56.03)

ACKNOWLEDGEMENTS

Thanks are due to the generosity of the gardeners in this book who not only allowed me to visit their gardens but who gave me introductions to other gardeners.

I should also like to thank the following people for giving me their time or advice: Barbara Abbs, Louis Benech, Georges Berniers, Richard Binns, Yves Bouedec, Betty and Olivia Chubb, Jo Dunn, Jerry Harpur, Clive and Meg Jones, Dr Louisa Dupont Jones, Robert Mallet, Gillian Mawrey, Mondes et Merveilles, Liz Robinson, Kathie Swift, Caroline Taylor, Mr and Mrs Taylor-Whitehead, David Wheeler.

To Georges Lévêque for his enthusiasm in following up all my gardens, some of which were well outside his usual province.

Finally Tamsin, for her patience, map-reading, driving and elegant French when telephoning unknown gardeners. Her encouragement, whenever I felt confused or in despair, was an unwavering support.

INDEX